Polished Spiral Karin Kuhlmann

"Although the creation of fractals is bounded to strict mathematical rules, the results are always very inspiring." – **Karin Kuhlmann**

Investigations
IN NUMBER, DATA, AND SPACE®

Editorial offices: Glenview, Illinois • Parsippany, New Jersey • New York, New York
Sales offices: Boston, Massachusetts • Duluth, Georgia
Glenview, Illinois • Coppell, Texas • Sacramento, California • Mesa, Arizona

The Investigations curriculum was developed by TERC, Cambridge, MA.

This material is based on work supported by the National Science Foundation ("NSF") under Grant No. ESI-0095450. Any opinions, findings, and conclusions or recommendations expressed in this material are those of the author(s) and do not necessarily reflect the views of the National Science Foundation.

ISBN: 0-328-24054-0

ISBN: 978-0-328-24054-8

5 6 7 8 9 10-V031-15 14 13 12 11 10 09 08

CC:N3

Polished Spiral Karin Kuhlmann

"Although the creation of fractals is bounded to strict mathematical rules, the results are always very inspiring." – **Karin Kuhlmann**

Investigations
IN NUMBER, DATA, AND SPACE®

© Pearson Education 4

Factors, Multiples, and Arrays

Investigation 3

How Many in This Array?

ORANGE JUICE

How many cans are in this case,
including those under the cap? _____48_____

How did you figure this out?

I count All the can including the ones
upunder the cap

Things That Come in Arrays

Think of things that come in arrays. For each thing you think of, fill in all four columns of the chart.

What Is It?	How Many in the Array?	Dimensions	Drawing of the Array
Black crake	8	4→ 2↓	
The cubes	6	2→ 3↓	
Lights	8	4→ 2↓	

Addition Starter Problems

Solve each problem in two different
ways, using the first steps given.
Show your work clearly.

> **NOTE** Students practice strategies
> for addition. They work on efficiency
> and flexibility by solving the same
> problem in two different ways.
>
> **SMH** 8–9

1. 254 + 763 = _____ **a.** Start by solving 200 + 700.	**b.** Start by solving 250 + 750.
2. 627 + 575 = _____ **a.** Start by solving 600 + 575.	**b.** Start by solving 27 + 75.

Ongoing Review

3. Find the missing number: 160, 260, 360, 460, _____

    A. 860   **B.** 560   **C.** 500   **D.** 480

Factors, Multiples, and Arrays

Looking at Our Arrays

As you walk around and look at our class arrays, answer the following questions:

1. Which numbers have only one array?

2. Which numbers have a square array?

3. Which numbers have the most arrays?

Array Picture Problems (page 1 of 2)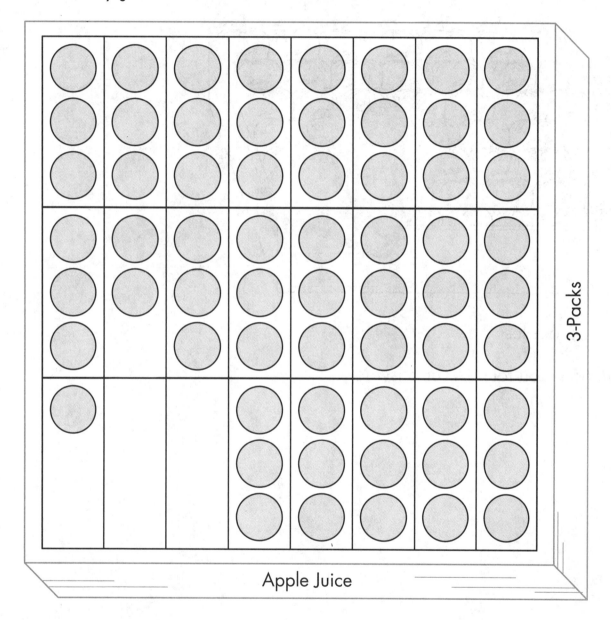

Problem A

How many juice cans were in this case when it was full?

3-Packs

Apple Juice

_____ juice cans

Explain how you found your answer.

Name _____   Date _____

Array Picture Problems (page 2 of 2)

Problem B

How many apples are in this case?

_____ apples

Explain how you found your answer.

Solve Two Ways

Solve this problem in two different ways. Be sure to record the equations and representations that show how you got your answer.

463 + 589 = _____

1. Here is the first way I solved it:

2. Here is the second way I solved it:

Ongoing Review

3. What is the total cost of a pennant and a cap?

A. $6.75   **C.** $13.99

B. $11.24   **D.** $14.99

Souvenirs	
Pennant	$4.50
Cap	$9.49
Ball	$2.25

More Things That Come in Groups

NOTE Students practice multiplication in a story problem context.

SMH 16–17

Solve these story problems. Write a multiplication equation for each problem and show how you solved it.

A week has 7 days.

1. How many days are in 4 weeks? _____

     Equation: _____

2. How many days are in 8 weeks? _____

     Equation: _____

3. How many days are in 12 weeks? _____

     Equation: _____

Collecting 1,000 Pennies

NOTE Students practice solving problems about the difference between three-digit numbers and 1,000.

Solve these problems. Be sure to write the equations that show how you got your answers.

The students in Ms. Shapiro's class want to collect 1,000 pennies in one month.

1. After the first week, they had collected 267 pennies. How many more do they need to collect to reach 1,000?

2. After two weeks, they had collected a total of 516 pennies. How many more do they now need to reach 1,000?

3. After 3 weeks, they had collected a total of 843 pennies. How many more do they need to collect in the last week to reach 1,000?

Related Problem Sets

Solve the related problems in each set. As you work on these problems, think about how solving the first problem in each set may help you solve the others.

NOTE Students solve addition and subtraction problems in related sets.

SMH 8, 9, 13–15

1. $\begin{array}{r} 500 \\ -\ 85 \\ \hline \end{array}$ $\begin{array}{r} 500 \\ -185 \\ \hline \end{array}$ $\begin{array}{r} 500 \\ -187 \\ \hline \end{array}$

2. $400 - 200 =$ _____

    $400 - 180 =$ _____

    $420 - 180 =$ _____

3. $300 - 150 =$ _____

    $350 - 150 =$ _____

    $353 - 150 =$ _____

    $353 - 147 =$ _____

4. $189 - 55 =$ _____

    $189 - 155 =$ _____

    $289 - 155 =$ _____

    $289 - 165 =$ _____

5. $600 +$ _____ $= 1,000$

    $650 +$ _____ $= 1,000$

    $655 +$ _____ $= 1,000$

    $658 +$ _____ $= 1,000$

6. $\begin{array}{r} 300 \\ 300 \\ +300 \\ \hline \end{array}$ $\begin{array}{r} 305 \\ 299 \\ +296 \\ \hline \end{array}$ $\begin{array}{r} 299 \\ 296 \\ +290 \\ \hline \end{array}$

Ongoing Review

7. Which does **not** equal 404?

    A. $199 + 205$ **B.** $201 + 203$ **C.** $198 + 202$ **D.** $202 + 202$

What's on the Other Side? (page 1 of 2)

For each of the two Array Cards shown, figure out the number of squares in the array. Explain how you solved each problem.

NOTE Students have been solving multiplication problems by using Array Cards. Here, students find the total number of units in the array and explain how they found it.

SMH 18–19

How did you solve 8 × 8?

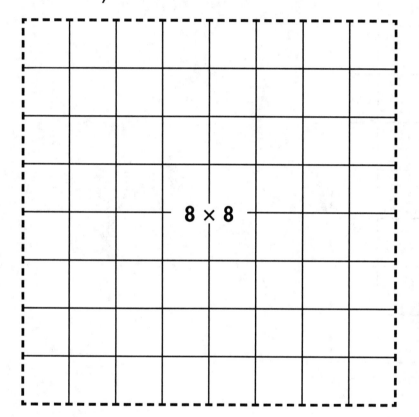

What's on the Other Side? (page 2 of 2)

How did you solve 7 × 9?

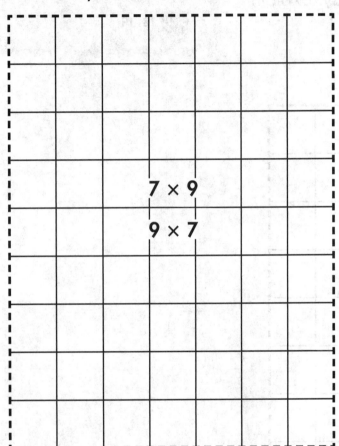

7 × 9

9 × 7

Multiple Turn Over Recording Sheet

Write the numbers of your 10 Multiple Cards on the blank cards. As each factor is called, record it in the factor list. Then write which multiples of that number you have among your cards.

Game 1   Multiple Cards

☐ ☐ ☐ ☐ ☐ ☐ ☐ ☐ ☐ ☐

Factor   **Multiple Cards I Can Turn Over**

1. _____   _____

2. _____   _____

3. _____   _____

4. _____   _____

5. _____   _____

Game 2   Multiple Cards

☐ ☐ ☐ ☐ ☐ ☐ ☐ ☐ ☐ ☐

Factor   **Multiple Cards I Can Turn Over**

1. _____   _____

2. _____   _____

3. _____   _____

4. _____   _____

5. _____   _____

Distance Problems

NOTE Students practice addition in a story problem context, finding a combination of addends that equals a given sum.

1. **a.** Elena's family is taking a bicycle vacation over 4 days. They plan to bicycle 115 miles in all. Write an addition equation that shows one possible combination of miles they could bike over 4 days.

   _____ + _____ + _____ + _____ = 115

   b. Write another equation to show a second way they could bike a total of 115 miles.

   _____ + _____ + _____ + _____ = 115

2. **a.** Edwin and his family are driving to a family reunion 516 miles away. They have 3 days to drive the total distance. Write an addition equation that shows one possible combination of miles they could drive over 3 days.

   _____ + _____ + _____ = 516

   b. Write another equation to show a second way they could drive a total of 516 miles.

   _____ + _____ + _____ = 516

Ongoing Review

3. 124 + 127 + 125 = _____

   A. 376   **B.** 375   **C.** 372   **D.** 366

Practicing with Multiplication Cards (page 1 of 2)

NOTE Students are learning the multiplication combinations (or "facts") up to 12 × 12. Help your child practice these.

SMH 29–34

1. Look at the front of each Multiplication Card. If you have a helper, that person can show you one card at a time.

2. Your job is to say the answer to the problem as quickly as you can. If you get the answer right away, put the card in a pile of combinations that you "just know." If you have to stop and figure it out, put it into a different pile of combinations that you are still "working on."

3. Paper-clip your "just know" cards together, and set them aside.

4. Look at each card in your "working on" pile. Think of an easy multiplication combination, one that you already know, that can help you remember each one. Write it on the line that says "Start with _____."

   Example: "For 6 × 7, I know that 7 × 7 = 49, so it must be one 7 less—that's 42."

$$6 \times 7$$
$$7 \times 6$$
Start with $\underline{\quad 7 \times 7 \quad}$

5. Go through each of the cards in your "working on" pile at least 3 times, using your "start with" combinations to help you find the answers.

6. Put all of your cards back together, both "just know" and "working on," and go through them again.

7. Over the next few weeks, keep practicing until you have no more cards in your "working on" pile. Practice at school when you have extra time, and practice at home with a family member.

Practicing with Multiplication Cards (page 2 of 2)

1. Which multiplication combinations are you practicing?

_____   _____

_____   _____

_____   _____

_____   _____

2. Write two multiplication combinations that are hard for you, and explain what helps you remember them.

Multiplication combination: _____

What helps me:

_____

_____

_____

Multiplication combination: _____

What helps me:

_____

_____

_____

3. How did you practice your multiplication combinations? Who helped you?

_____

_____

_____

_____

Money Problems

Solve these problems. Show clearly how you
solved each one.

NOTE Students practice
addition and subtraction in
the context of money.

SMH **8, 9, 13, 14, 15**

1. $6.57 + $4.98 = _____

2. $7.34 + $2.78 = _____

3. $8.60 − $3.95 = _____

4. $7.30 − $4.75 = _____

Ongoing Review

5. One pen costs $1.55. What is the total cost of 3 pens?

A. $3.65   **B.** $4.55   **C.** $4.65   **D.** $5.55

Name _____   Date _____

Factors, Multiples, and Arrays   **Homework**

More Practice with Multiplication Cards

NOTE Students are learning the multiplication combinations (multiplication "facts") to 12 × 12. Continue helping your child with this practice.

SMH 29–34

1. Which multiplication combinations are you practicing?

_____   _____

_____   _____

_____   _____

2. Write two multiplication combinations that are hard for you, and explain what helps you remember them.

Multiplication combination: _____

What helps me:

_____

_____

_____

Multiplication combination: _____

What helps me:

_____

_____

_____

3. How did you practice your multiplication combinations? Who helped you?

_____

_____

_____

         Session 2.4

Picnic Supplies

Solve these problems. Be sure to write the equations that show how you got your answers.

NOTE Students solve addition and subtraction problems in a story problem context.

SMH 8–9, 13–15

1. The Cottonwood School is having a school picnic. The school brought 400 bottles of juice, and students drank 318 of them at the picnic. How many bottles of juice were left over?

2. There are 143 plates left over from last year's picnic, and the principal wants a total of 500 plates. How many more plates does the principal need?

3. The school provides 117 apples, 241 oranges, 86 bananas, and 43 pears. How many pieces of fruit are there in all?

4. This year 463 people came to the picnic. Last year, because of cold weather, only 227 came. How many more people came to this year's picnic?

Factors and Products

Fill in the chart with the missing factors or products.

NOTE Students are working to become fluent with multiplication combinations (also called multiplication "facts"). Here, they practice multiplication combinations by finding products or missing factors.

SMH **26, 29–34**

Factor	×	Factor	=	Product
	×	8	=	16
4	×	7	=	
6	×		=	24
	×	5	=	30
3	×	9	=	
7	×		=	49
8	×	6	=	
10	×		=	100
	×	4	=	36

Finding the Factors of 100

Find the factors of 100. You may use the 100 chart, cubes, arrays, grid paper, or drawings to help you make sure that the numbers you choose are factors. Record the factors in the chart.

Factor	How Many in 100?	Factor Pair
Example: 1	100	100 × 1

When you think you have found all of the factors of 100, list them here.

_____

_____

_____

Factors, Multiples, and Arrays

Finding the Factors of 200

Find the factors of 200. Record the factors in the chart. You can use multiplication combinations you know to help you. You can also use the 200 chart, cubes, arrays, grid paper, or drawings to find the factors.

Factor	How Many in 200?	Factor Pair	Factor	How Many in 200?	Factor Pair

When you think you have found all of the factors of 200, list them here.

_____

_____

_____

Finding the Factors of 300

Find the factors of 300. Record the factors in the chart.
You can use multiplication combinations you know to help
you. You can also use the 300 chart, cubes, arrays, grid
paper, or drawings to find the factors.

Factor	How Many in 300?	Factor Pair	Factor	How Many in 300?	Factor Pair

When you think you have found all of the factors of 300,
list them here.

_____

_____

_____

How Many More?

Solve these problems. Show your solutions on the number lines provided.

NOTE Students find the missing number to make a correct addition equation.

1. $621 + \underline{\hspace{1.5cm}} = 950$

2. $481 + \underline{\hspace{1.5cm}} = 895$

3. $508 + \underline{\hspace{1.5cm}} = 780$

4. $437 + \underline{\hspace{1.5cm}} = 1,100$

More Factors and Products

Fill in the chart with the missing factors
or products.

> **NOTE** Students are working to become fluent with multiplication combinations (also called multiplication "facts"). Here, they solve problems to find a factor or products in some of the more difficult combinations.
>
> **SMH** 26, 29–34

Factor	×	Factor	=	Product
10	×	9	=	
	×	7	=	77
12	×	8	=	
9	×		=	63
8	×	9	=	
	×	6	=	42
5	×	8	=	
6	×		=	48
4	×		=	36

Finding the Factors of Other Multiples of 100 (page 1 of 2)

Choose a multiple of 100 that is greater than 300, such as 400, 500, or 600. Write this number in the blank below, "How Many in _____?" Record the factors of that number in the chart. Use multiplication combinations you know to help you. You can also use the 300 chart, cubes, arrays, grid paper, or drawings.

Factor	How Many in _____?	Factor Pair	Factor	How Many in _____?	Factor Pair

When you think you have found all of the factors of this multiple, list them here.

_____

_____

Finding the Factors of Other Multiples of 100 (page 2 of 2)

Now choose another multiple of 100 that is greater than 300.
Record the factors of that number in the chart. Keep using
multiplication combinations you know to help you, along with
the 300 chart, cubes, arrays, grid paper, or drawings.

Factor	How Many in ____?	Factor Pair	Factor	How Many in ____?	Factor Pair

When you think you have found all of the factors of this
multiple, list them here.

_____

_____

_____

Story Problems

Solve these problems. Show how you got
your answers.

NOTE Students solve
multistep addition and
subtraction problems in
a story problem context.

SMH **8–9, 13–15**

1. Marisa had 574 stamps in her stamp collection.
   She gave 255 stamps to her brother to start his
   own collection. Then Marisa's aunt gave her
   449 stamps. How many stamps does Marisa
   have in her collection now?

2. Ms. Gomez is running for the city council. She printed
   1,000 campaign brochures for the elections. On the first
   day, she gave away 387 brochures. On the second day,
   she gave away 515 brochures. How many brochures
   does she have left?

3. **a.** Devon earned $13.50 for babysitting his niece. He
      also earned $4.50 for doing his chores that week.
      He wants to buy a backpack that costs $18.45.
      Does he have enough money?

   b. If he does not have enough money, how much more
      does he need?

Factors of Multiples of 100 (page 1 of 2)

Fill in each chart on these two pages. Tell how many of the given factor it takes to get to each multiple of 100. Then write the factor pair. Look at the first two charts for examples. Use multiplication combinations you know, or use math tools, such as the 300 chart, to help you.

NOTE Students are working on finding factors of 100, 200, 300, and other multiples of 100. Here, they find ways to multiply to make these numbers.

SMH 26

Factor	How Many?	Multiple	Factor Pair	Factor	How Many?	Multiple	Factor Pair
2	50	100	2 × 50	5	20	100	5 × 20
2		200		5		200	
2		300		5		300	
2		400		5		400	
2		500		5		500	
2		600		5		600	

Name   Date

Factors, Multiples, and Arrays   Homework

Factors of Multiples
of 100 (page 2 of 2)

Continue filling in these charts. Remember, you can use
multiplication combinations you know or math tools, such
as the 300 chart, to help you.

Factor	How Many?	Multiple	Factor Pair	Factor	How Many?	Multiple	Factor Pair
10		100		20		100	
10		200		20		200	
10		300		20		300	
10		400		20		400	
10		500		20		500	
10		600		20		600	

Factor	How Many?	Multiple	Factor Pair	Factor	How Many?	Multiple	Factor Pair
25	4	100	25 × 4	4	25	100	4 × 25
25		200		4		200	
25		300		4		300	
25		400		4		400	
25		500		4		500	
25		600		4		600	

Factors, Multiples, and Arrays

How Many People Counted?

Read the problems, and answer the questions. Try to solve the problems without actually doing the skip counting yourself. What do you know that will help you?

> **NOTE** Students have been finding the multiples of given numbers in a routine called Counting Around the Class (for example, 20, 40, 60, 80, . . .). Here, they practice finding a series of multiples of a number.
>
> **SMH** 24, 25

1. Ms. McCoy's class counted by 20s. How many people counted to get to 300? How do you know?

2. Mr. Harris's class counted by 10s. How many people counted to get to 300? How do you know?

3. Ms. Gomez's class counted by 25s. How many people counted to get to 300? How do you know?

Factors, Multiples, and Arrays

Factors of 16 and 48 (page 1 of 2)

1. Find the factors of 16 and the factors of 48. Use arrays, pictures, or cubes to show your thinking.

Factors of 16:

Factors of 48:

Factors of 16 and 48 (page 2 of 2)

2. Explain why all of the factors of 16 are also factors of 48. Use arrays, pictures, or cubes to help you make your argument.

3. 32 and 64 are multiples of 16.

   $2 \times 16 = 32$

   $4 \times 16 = 64$

   Choose one of the factors of 16, and find out whether it is also a factor of 32 and 64. Do you think all of the factors of 16 are also factors of the multiples of 32 and 64? Are the factors of 16 also factors of other multiples of 16? Explain your thinking.

Combinations to 100 and 200

NOTE Students use number sense and place-value knowledge to solve addition problems.

1. [4] [9] [2] [7] [6] [3]

[ ] [ ] + [ ] [ ] = _____

Use this set of digits to write an equation that will be as close to 100 as possible. Use 2-digit numbers in your equation. Explain why this is as close to 100 as you can get with this set of digits.

2. [4] [9] [2] [7] [6] [3] [5] [1]

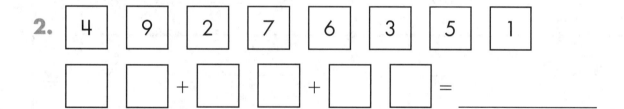

Use this set of digits to write an equation that will be as close to 200 as possible. Use three 2-digit numbers in your equation. Explain why this is as close to 200 as you can get with this set of digits.

Multiplying by Factors of 100

Solve each set of problems. Look for patterns that might help you.

NOTE Students have been finding factors of 100, 200, and 300. Here, they solve multiplication problems that involve these factors.

SMH **37, 38**

1. $2 \times 50 =$ _____

$4 \times 50 =$ _____

$6 \times 50 =$ _____

2. $4 \times 25 =$ _____

$6 \times 25 =$ _____

$8 \times 25 =$ _____

3. _____ $\times 4 = 100$

_____ $\times 4 = 200$

_____ $\times 4 = 300$

4. $10 \times$ _____ $= 200$

$10 \times$ _____ $= 300$

$10 \times$ _____ $= 400$

5. $5 \times 20 =$ _____

$10 \times 20 =$ _____

$15 \times 20 =$ _____

6. _____ $\times 5 = 100$

_____ $\times 5 = 200$

_____ $\times 5 = 400$

Name _____ Date _____

Rock On!

Solve each problem. Draw the arrays and write equations. Use another sheet of paper if you need to.

> **NOTE** Students solve real-world problems involving the math content of this unit.
>
> **SMH** 18–21

1. Rock bands often stack their speakers in an array. One teen band has 24 speakers. They stack them at least 2 high, but no taller than 8 high. What are all the different arrays they can make?

2. One band has 30 speakers. They stack them at least 3 high, but no taller than 6 high. What are all the different arrays they could make?

3. Another band has 48 speakers. They stack them at least 4 high, but no taller than 6 high. What are all the different arrays they can make?

4. One band has fewer than 40 speakers. They stack them in an array exactly 9 high. How many speakers could they have? Explain how you know.

Polished Spiral Karin Kuhlmann

"Although the creation of fractals is bounded to strict mathematical rules, the results are always very inspiring." – **Karin Kuhlmann**

Investigations
IN NUMBER, DATA, AND SPACE®

Describing the Shape of the Data

Multiplication Combinations of 3s, 6s, and 12s

NOTE: Students practice multiplication combinations ("facts"). They look for patterns in the 3s, 6s, and 12s combinations.

SMH 29–34

1. Solve these problems.

$1 \times 3 =$

$2 \times 3 =$ $1 \times 6 =$

$3 \times 3 =$

$4 \times 3 =$ $2 \times 6 =$ $1 \times 12 =$

$5 \times 3 =$

$6 \times 3 =$ $3 \times 6 =$

$7 \times 3 =$

$8 \times 3 =$ $4 \times 6 =$ $2 \times 12 =$

$9 \times 3 =$

$10 \times 3 =$ $5 \times 6 =$

$11 \times 3 =$

$12 \times 3 =$ $6 \times 6 =$ $3 \times 12 =$

2. What patterns do you notice?

3. Ask someone at home to help you practice the multiplication combinations that you are working on.

Party Supplies

NOTE Students practice solving multiplication problems in a story context.

Solve each of the story problems below.
Show your thinking.

1. Ms. Ruiz bought 13 packages of cups for a big party. Each package contains 8 cups. How many cups did she buy?

2. Ms. Ruiz bought 9 packages of plates for the party. Each package contains 12 plates. How many plates did she buy?

3. Ms. Ruiz bought 7 packages of napkins for the party. Each package contains 16 napkins. How many napkins did she buy?

Ongoing Review

4. Which product is greater than 70?

   A. 7×9 **C.** 5×11

   B. 6×12 **D.** 8×8

Related Multiplication Combinations

Solve each set of related problems below.

NOTE Students solve sets of related multiplication combinations. Encourage them to solve each problem mentally.

 SMH 29–34

1. $5 \times 7 =$ _____ $10 \times 7 =$ _____	**2.** $9 \times 10 =$ _____ $9 \times 12 =$ _____	**3.** $7 \times 6 =$ _____ $7 \times 7 =$ _____
4. $4 \times 8 =$ _____ $8 \times 8 =$ _____ $12 \times 8 =$ _____	**5.** $4 \times 6 =$ _____ $8 \times 6 =$ _____ $12 \times 6 =$ _____	**6.** $6 \times 8 =$ _____ $7 \times 8 =$ _____ $8 \times 8 =$ _____
7. $10 \times 10 =$ _____ $11 \times 11 =$ _____ $12 \times 12 =$ _____	**8.** $12 \times 3 =$ _____ $12 \times 6 =$ _____ $12 \times 9 =$ _____	**9.** $6 \times 6 =$ _____ $8 \times 6 =$ _____ $10 \times 6 =$ _____
10. $11 \times 4 =$ _____ $11 \times 6 =$ _____ $11 \times 10 =$ _____	**11.** $7 \times 5 =$ _____ $7 \times 6 =$ _____ $7 \times 11 =$ _____	**12.** $9 \times 5 =$ _____ $9 \times 7 =$ _____ $9 \times 9 =$ _____

Factors

For each of the following numbers, list as many pairs of factors as you can.

NOTE Students practice multiplication combinations ("facts") by finding pairs of factors for a given product.

SMH 22, 23

Example: 28

    2 × 14

    4 × 7

    ____ × ____

24

____ × ____

____ × ____

____ × ____

32

____ × ____

____ × ____

____ × ____

18

____ × ____

____ × ____

____ × ____

16

____ × ____

____ × ____

____ × ____

20

____ × ____

____ × ____

____ × ____

How Many Cavities?

How many cavities have you had?

NOTE Students are gathering data about the number of cavities they have had for a class data collection.

SMH **87**

Comparing the Heights of First and Fourth Graders ✏️WRITING

1. How do the heights of the first-graders compare with the heights of the fourth graders in your class? Write three statements about this question.

   In your statements include ideas about the data such as these: Where are there lots of data? How big are clumps of data? What are the tallest heights and the shortest heights? What outliers are there? What do you think are the typical heights of first graders and of fourth graders?

   a. _____

   b. _____

   c. _____

2. About how much taller do you think a fourth grader is than a first grader? Why do you think so? Support your ideas with evidence from the data.

   _____

   _____

   _____

   _____

   _____

   _____

Counting Around the Class

NOTE Students find the multiples of a given number and solve multiplication problems.

 25

1. Mr. Patel's students counted by 5s. The first person said 5, the second said 10, and the third said 15. Each student said one number. How many students counted to get to 100? _____
How do you know?

2. Ms. Bailey's students counted by 10s. The first person said 10, the second said 20, and the third said 30. Each student said one number.

   a. How many students counted to get to 270? _____
   How do you know?

   b. When Ms. Bailey's students counted by 10s, did anyone say the number 225? _____
   How do you know?

Ongoing Review

3. Which has the same product as 3 × 12?

   A. 8 × 4   **C.** 6 × 6

   B. 6 × 24   **D.** 9 × 6

Things That Come in Groups

Solve the story problems below. Write a multiplication equation for each problem and show how you solved it.

NOTE Students practice multiplication by solving story problems.

 16, 17

Spiders have 8 legs.

1. How many legs are on 5 spiders? _____

Equation: _____$5 \times 8 =$_____

2. How many legs are on 11 spiders? _____

Equation: _____

3. How many legs are on 16 spiders? _____

Equation: _____

Ongoing Review

4. Which is **not** a factor of 54?

    A. 3   **C.** 8

    B. 6   **D.** 9

Developing a Survey Question (page 1 of 3)

1. Choose a survey question.

   Think about a question that will:
   - Help you compare two groups of people.
   - Result in numerical data.
   - Give you data that you are interested in.
   - Help you find out something that you don't know.

   Decide on a question for your survey. Write your question.

   _____

   _____

2. Try out and revise your question.

   Ask three students your survey question. Talk with them and your partner about making changes to your question.

   Think about the following:
   - Did the students understand your question?
   - Were they able to respond to your question without further explanation from you?
   - Did their responses give you the information you were interested in?

   If you revise your question, write it here.

   _____

   _____

Developing a Survey Question (page 2 of 3)

3. Plan your survey and make predictions.

   a. You will compare the responses to your question from two groups of students. Which two groups of students will you compare?

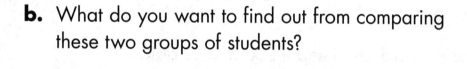

   b. What do you want to find out from comparing these two groups of students?

_____

_____

_____

_____

   c. What do you predict you will find when you compare the responses of these two groups of students? Why do you think this will be the result?

_____

_____

_____

Developing a Survey Question (page 3 of 3)

4. Plan how to collect and record your data.

Think about the following:

- How are you going to record the data as you collect them?
- What information do you need to write?
- How are you going to keep track of which people you have asked?
- Who is going to do what?

Write how you will record and keep track of your data.

_____

_____

_____

_____

_____

_____

Peanut Count

NOTE Students represent data in a line plot.

SMH **88–89**

Each of the students in Mr. Herrera's class took a handful of trail mix and counted the number of peanuts.

1. Make a line plot of the data.

Peanut Count			
Benson	8	Yuson	6
Yuki	5	Anna	7
Noemi	6	Helena	9
Derek	13	LaTanya	8
Bill	10	Marisol	9
Abdul	9	Andrew	8
Steve	8	Ursula	10
Damian	8	Sabrina	6
Lucy	8	Richard	6

2. If you took a handful of the same trail mix, how many peanuts do you think you would get? Explain why you think so.

_____

_____

Ongoing Review

3. What is the highest number of peanuts a student counted?

A. 13   **B.** 7   **C.** 6   **D.** 5

14 Unit 2

How Many Cubes Can Students Grab? (page 1 of 2)

Students in a third-grade class collected data about how many cubes kindergarteners and third graders could grab with one hand. They put their data in two bar graphs.

NOTE In this homework, students look carefully at the shapes of two different sets of data and compare them.

SMH **94–97**

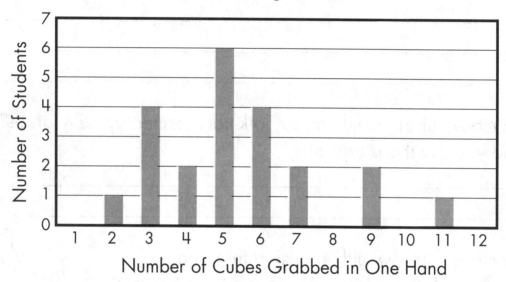

Kindergarteners

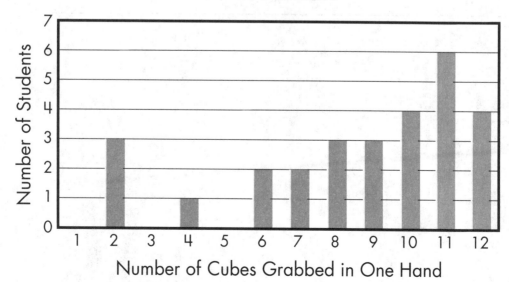

Third Graders

How Many Cubes Can Students Grab? (page 2 of 2)

1. Write three statements about the number of cubes
third graders and kindergartners grabbed.

a. _____

_____

b. _____

_____

c. _____

_____

2. How many cubes would you say a kindergartner typically grabs? Why
would you say this is typical?

_____

_____

3. How many cubes would you say a third grader
typically grabs? Why would you say this is typical?

_____

_____

Interesting Plot

Ollie counted the number of houses on each block between home and school. The line plot shows Ollie's data.

NOTE Students describe features of a set of data on a line plot.

SMH 88, 89, 90, 91

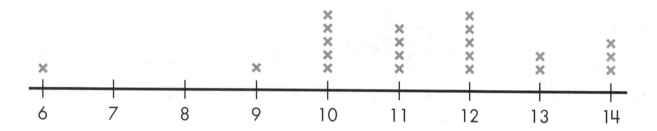

1. What seems to be the typical number of houses? Explain why you think so.

_____

_____

_____

_____

2. An *outlier* is a piece of data that "lies outside" the rest of the data. Are there any outliers? If so, what is it and what might account for this unusual piece of data?

_____

_____

_____

Ongoing Review

3. How many blocks have 11 houses?

    A. 1   **B.** 2   **C.** 3   **D.** 4

Name _____ Date _____

Homework

Missing Factors

Fill in the missing factors in these problems.

NOTE Students practice multiplication combinations ("facts") in related sets.

 29–34

1.

$6 \times$ _____ $= 36$

$6 \times$ _____ $= 72$

2.

$9 \times$ _____ $= 36$

$9 \times$ _____ $= 72$

3.

_____ $\times 12 = 36$

_____ $\times 12 = 72$

4.

_____ $\times 8 = 48$

_____ $\times 8 = 88$

5.

$11 \times$ _____ $= 44$

$11 \times$ _____ $= 88$

6.

$6 \times$ _____ $= 48$

$6 \times$ _____ $= 54$

7.

$9 \times$ _____ $= 45$

$9 \times$ _____ $= 54$

$9 \times$ _____ $= 63$

8.

_____ $\times 7 = 21$

_____ $\times 7 = 42$

_____ $\times 7 = 84$

9.

_____ $\times 8 = 40$

_____ $\times 8 = 48$

_____ $\times 8 = 56$

10.

$7 \times$ _____ $= 28$

$7 \times$ _____ $= 35$

$7 \times$ _____ $= 63$

11.

$6 \times$ _____ $= 36$

$8 \times$ _____ $= 64$

$12 \times$ _____ $= 144$

12.

_____ $\times 12 = 48$

_____ $\times 12 = 60$

_____ $\times 12 = 108$

Related Multiplication Combinations

Solve the following problems.

NOTE Students practice multiplication combinations ("facts") in related sets.

 SMH 29–34

1.	2.	3.
$5 \times 8 =$ _____	$11 \times 10 =$ _____	$7 \times 4 =$ _____
$10 \times 8 =$ _____	$11 \times 12 =$ _____	$7 \times 8 =$ _____

4.	5.	6.
$4 \times 6 =$ _____	$4 \times 9 =$ _____	$6 \times 6 =$ _____
$8 \times 6 =$ _____	$8 \times 9 =$ _____	$7 \times 7 =$ _____
$12 \times 6 =$ _____	$12 \times 9 =$ _____	$8 \times 8 =$ _____

7.	8.	9.
$10 \times 12 =$ _____	$8 \times 3 =$ _____	$6 \times 6 =$ _____
$11 \times 12 =$ _____	$8 \times 6 =$ _____	$8 \times 6 =$ _____
$12 \times 12 =$ _____	$8 \times 9 =$ _____	$10 \times 6 =$ _____

10.	11.	12.
$11 \times 5 =$ _____	$7 \times 5 =$ _____	$12 \times 5 =$ _____
$11 \times 6 =$ _____	$7 \times 6 =$ _____	$12 \times 7 =$ _____
$11 \times 11 =$ _____	$7 \times 12 =$ _____	$12 \times 9 =$ _____

Name _____   Date _____

What Did You Learn From Your Survey? (page 1 of 2)

1. What was your survey question?

_____

_____

2. Suppose that a teacher was interested in your survey
and asked, "What did you learn from your survey?"
Write at least three things you learned. Give evidence
from the data.

_____

_____

_____

_____

_____

_____

_____

What Did You Learn From Your Survey? (page 2 of 2)

3. How did the results of your survey compare with your predictions?

_____

_____

_____

_____

4. Now that you have learned some things about your question, can you think of some other survey questions that you would ask to learn more about this topic?

_____

_____

_____

_____

_____

5. What else did you learn about data investigations from doing this project?

_____

_____

_____

_____

Division With Remainders

NOTE Students practice solving division problems and interpreting remainders in story problem contexts.

 47, 48–49

1. Fifty people are waiting in line for the roller coaster. Each car holds 8 people. How many cars will the 50 people fill?

   Division equation: _____ ÷ _____ = _____   Answer: _____

2. Forty people bought tickets for a boat ride. Twelve people can ride in a boat at a time. How many boats will the 40 people fill?

   Division equation: _____ ÷ _____ = _____   Answer: _____

3. How many prizes could you get with 50 tickets?

   Division equation:

   _____ ÷ _____ = _____

   Answer: _____

ARCADE PRIZES

6 Tickets per prize!

4. The students in Mr. Brown's class counted around the class by 5s. Each student said one number. The number they ended with was 65. How many students counted?

   Division equation: _____ ÷ _____ = _____   Answer: _____

Ongoing Review

5. The students in Ms. Jones' class counted around the class by 4s. Each student said one number. There are 29 students in her class. Which of these numbers did they say?

   A. 120   **B.** 100   **C.** 50   **D.** 10

Arranging Cans of Juice (page 1 of 2)

NOTE Students find factors by arranging numbers into rectangular arrays.

SMH **18, 23**

Solve the following problems.

1. **a.** You have 28 cans of juice. Show all of the ways you can arrange these cans into arrays. Draw the arrays in the space below.

b. List all of the factors of 28.

Arranging Cans of Juice (page 2 of 2)

2. a. Mauricio has 42 cans of juice. Show all of the ways he can arrange his cans into arrays. Draw the arrays in the space below.

b. List all of the factors of 42.

Mystery Data A

The table and graph below show the same data.
These data represent some group of living things.

Individual	Inches	Individual	Inches	Individual	Inches
A	84	I	84	Q	81
B	83	J	84	R	79
C	78	K	85	S	75
D	75	L	82	T	76
E	90	M	78	U	83
F	77	N	83	V	81
G	75	O	72	W	78
H	81	P	80	X	78

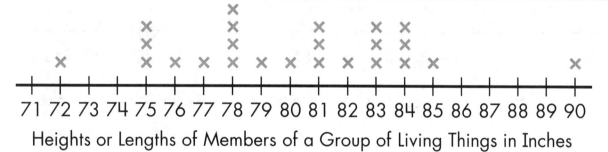

Heights or Lengths of Members of a Group of Living Things in Inches

1. What is the median height or length of this group?
    Are the data clustered around the median or spread out?

    _____

    _____

2. What do you think the group could be? Give reasons
    for your answer.

    _____

    _____

    _____

Mystery Data B

The table and graph below show the same data.
These data represent some group of living things.

Individual	Inches	Individual	Inches	Individual	Inches
A	78	G	86	M	84
B	96	H	93	N	80
C	114	I	64	O	72
D	94	J	54	P	54
E	63	K	72	Q	79
F	72	L	108	R	116

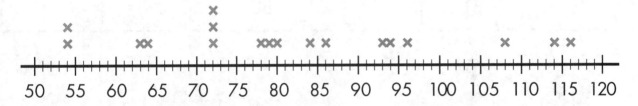

50 55 60 65 70 75 80 85 90 95 100 105 110 115 120

Heights or Lengths of Members of a Group of Living Things in Inches

1. What is the median height or length of this group?
   Are the data clustered around the median or spread out?

   _____

   _____

2. What do you think the group could be? Give reasons
   for your answer.

   _____

   _____

   _____

   _____

Mystery Data C

This information is about a group of living things:

- The median height or length of these living things is 19.5 inches.
- The shortest height or length in this group is 18 inches.
- The tallest height or length in this group is 22 inches.
- There are 30 individuals in this group.

1. Make a line plot of the heights or lengths of these living things. Decide where you think the 30 pieces of data might belong, according to the information above.

2. What do you think the group could be? Give reasons for your answer.

_____
_____
_____
_____
_____
_____

Parking Lot Data

The students in Ms. May's class counted the cars in the school parking lot at the beginning of every school day for a month.

NOTE Students represent and describe a set of data.

SMH **88–91**

1. Represent the data in a table, a line plot, or with tallies.

Number of Cars in the Parking Lot				
18	23	22	25	20
23	19	17	24	23
22	23	25	24	24
22	23	22	24	25

2. Describe the data. Try to include a discussion of the range, how it clumps or spreads out, whether there are any outliers, and what is typical.

_____

_____

_____

_____

Ongoing Review

3. What is the median number of cars in the parking lot?

   A. 20   **B.** 21   **C.** 22   **D.** 23

Things That Come in Groups

Solve the story problems below. Write a
multiplication equation for each problem,
and show how you solved it.

> **NOTE** Students solve multiplication problems and write an equation to represent each problem.
>
> SMH 16, 17

Insects have 6 legs.

1. How many legs do 9 insects have? _____

   Equation: _____

2. How many legs do 11 insects have? _____

   Equation: _____

3. How many legs do 20 insects have? _____

   Equation: _____

Comparing WNBA Players' Points Per Game (page 1 of 2)

Yolanda Griffith and Mwadi Mabika both played basketball in the WNBA (Women's National Basketball Association). They each scored points during most of the games they played in the 2003 season.

Here is a line plot of the points Mabika scored in each of the 40 games she played in the 2003 season:

Points Mabika Scored per Game

Below are the points Griffith scored during each of the 39 games she played in the 2003 season. Make a line plot of her points per game:

10 15 17 20 27 17 12 10 8 19 19 19 6 7 12 16 16 21
22 22 11 24 20 15 17 17 18 7 27 15 22 13 6 4 15 11 7

Points Griffith Scored per Game

Comparing WNBA Players' Points Per Game (page 2 of 2)

1. What is the median of Mabika's points per game? _____
How did you figure out the median?

_____

_____

_____

2. What is the median of Griffith's points per game? _____
How did you figure out the median?

_____

_____

_____

3. How do the number of points Griffith scored in the games she played in the 2003 season compare with the number of points Mabika scored? Write at least three statements that compare Mabika's points-per-game with Griffith's points-per-game.

Consider where the data are concentrated, the highest and lowest numbers of points scored, the outliers, and the medians.

1. _____

_____

2. _____

_____

3. _____

_____

How Heavy is Your Pumpkin?

NOTE Students practice representing and describing data.

SMH **88–93**

Damian grew eighteen pumpkins and recorded their weights when he picked them.

1. Organize the data in a line plot or other graph.

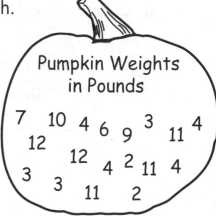

Pumpkin Weights in Pounds

7 10 4 6 9 3 11 4
12 12 4 2 11 4
3 3 11 2

2. Describe how the data is spread out by finding the median and other measures, such as the range. Discuss whether you think the median *alone* provides a good description of the data and why.

_____

_____

_____

_____

Ongoing Review

3. Half of the pumpkins weigh less than

A. 5 pounds   **B.** 4 pounds   **C.** 3 pounds   **D.** 2 pounds

Describing the Shape of the Data

Is This a Good Game? (page 1 of 2)

Use Mabika's and Griffith's points per game to answer the following questions.

1. Barney, who is a big fan of Mwadi Mabika, went to her game on May 28. Mabika scored 10 points. Barney wants to know whether this was a good game or a bad game for Mabika. What is your opinion? Use the data to support your opinion.

   _____

   _____

   _____

2. Venetta, who is a big fan of Yolanda Griffith, went to her game on July 5. Griffith scored 17 points. Venetta wants to know whether this was a good game or a bad game for Griffith. What is your opinion? Use the data to support your opinion.

   _____

   _____

   _____

3. Suppose that you were an owner of a team who was thinking about hiring Mwadi Mabika or Yolanda Griffith. As you decide whom to hire, one of the things you want to look at carefully is the player's points per game. According to their point scoring data, which player do you think you might hire for your basketball team? Why?

   _____

   _____

Is This a Good Game? (page 2 of 2)

4. Suppose that a sports reporter is writing a story comparing the points Yolanda Griffith and Mwadi Mabika scored during the 2003 season. The reporter is planning to report their median scores. What can the reporter's readers learn from a comparison of their median scores?

_____

_____

_____

_____

_____

_____

_____

5. Do you think this is enough information for readers to know about Griffith's and Mabika's scoring records? If not, what other information do you think the reporter should include?

_____

_____

_____

_____

_____

_____

_____

Multiplication Pairs

NOTE Students practice solving multiplication problems.

SMH 16–17

1. Solve each pair of multiplication problems below.

   Use the first problem to help you solve the second problem.

$12 \times 8 = $ _____	$15 \times 6 = $ _____
$24 \times 8 = $ _____	$30 \times 3 = $ _____
$15 \times 4 = $ _____	$9 \times 9 = $ _____
$15 \times 8 = $ _____	$18 \times 9 = $ _____
$32 \times 5 = $ _____	$8 \times 6 = $ _____
$16 \times 10 = $ _____	$16 \times 6 = $ _____

Ongoing Review

2. Which of the following does not equal 12×8?

   A. 24×4 **C.** 3×28

   B. 2×48 **D.** 6×16

Describing the Shape of the Data

Height Comparisons
(page 1 of 2)

A few days ago, you looked at some heights and lengths of different animals and people. Look at the following heights and lengths:

> **NOTE** Students use a set of data to answer questions about the lengths or heights of members of a group of living things.
>
> **SMH** 11–12

Names	Heights/Lengths
Vince Carter (basketball player)	78 inches
Shaquille O'Neal (basketball player)	85 inches
Baby 1	18 inches
Baby 2	22 inches
Fourth grader	64 inches
Shannon (boa constrictor)	116 inches
Black cottonwood (tree)	1,764 inches

1. Who is the taller basketball player? _____

   Who is the shorter baby? _____

   How much taller is the taller basketball player than the shorter baby? _____ Show your work.

Height Comparisons
(page 2 of 2)

2. Look at the fourth grader and Shannon. How
much longer is Shannon than the fourth grader
is tall? _____ Show your work.

3. How tall are you? _____ Find someone
or something that is at least 20" taller than you.
What is it? _____ How much taller
is it? _____ Show your work.

4. Look at the black cottonwood and the fourth grader.
How much taller is the black cottonwood than the fourth
grader? _____ Show your work.

How Many People Counted?

NOTE Students find the multiples of a given number and solve multiplication problems.

 25

In these counting problems, each student said one number.

1. The students in Ms. Alonzo's class counted by 20s. The first student said 20, the second student said 40, and the third said 60. How many students counted to get to 300? _____ How do you know?

2. The students in Mr. Nelson's class counted by 15s. The first student said 15, the second student said 30, and the third said 45. How many students counted to get to 300? _____ How do you know?

3. The students in Ms. Weinberg's class counted by 25s. The first student said 25, the second student said 50, and the third student said 75.

   a. How many students counted to get to 300? _____ How do you know?

   b. When the students in Ms. Weinberg's class counted by 25s, did anyone say the number 180? _____ How do you know?

Creating a Likelihood Line (page 1 of 2)

NOTE Students are beginning a study of probability. They are placing events according to their likelihood.

SMH **98**

Think about the neighborhood in which you live. Can you think of any events in the future that you are *certain* will happen? Write them on the likelihood line on the next page.

Add any events that would be *impossible*.

Now add a few events that are *unlikely* to occur, that *maybe* will occur, and that are *likely* to occur. You may want to ask family members or friends to help you think of events and where they might go on the line.

Now answer the questions below. Use examples from your Likelihood Line.

1. If something is unlikely to happen, does this mean that it will never happen? _____
   What would you think if it did happen?

   _____

   _____

   _____

2. If something is likely to happen, does this mean that it will always happen? _____
   What would you think if it did not happen?

   _____

   _____

   _____

   _____

Creating a Likelihood Line (page 2 of 2)

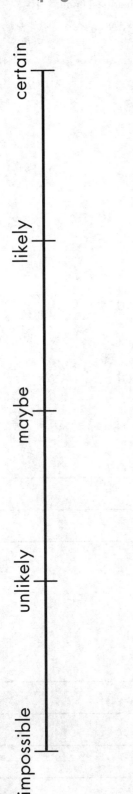

Placing Events on the Likelihood Line (page 1 of 2)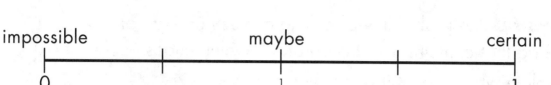

Put the letter of each event on the Likelihood Line above.
Explain your reasoning.

1. **Event A** The probability of flipping a coin and
   getting heads.
   Explain why you put it where you did.

   _____

   _____

2. **Event B** The probability of rolling a number cube and
   getting a 6.
   Explain why you put it where you did.

   _____

   _____

3. **Event C** The probability of rolling a number cube once
   and getting either a 1, a 2, or a 3.
   Explain why you put it where you did.

   _____

   _____

Placing Events on the Likelihood Line (page 2 of 2)

4. **Event D** the probability of pulling a blue cube out of a bag that contains 1 red cube and 99 blue cubes.

   Explain why you put it where you did.

   _____

   _____

5. **Event E** the probability of pulling a girl's name out of a container that holds the names of all of the students in the class.

   Explain why you put it where you did.

   _____

   _____

6. **Event F** the probability of pulling a boy's name out of the same container.

   Explain why you put it where you did.

   _____

   _____

7. **Event G** the probability of pulling your name out of the same container.

   Explain why you put it where you did.

   _____

   _____

Comparing Test Scores

These line plots show two students' scores for 12 science tests.

NOTE Students order and find the median of data sets.

SMH 92–93

Anna's Science Tests

Jill's Science Tests

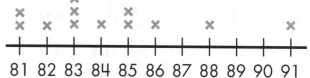

1. Find the median score for each student.

   Anna _____   Jill _____

2. Overall, which student do you think had better scores?

   _____

   Why do you think so?

   _____

   _____

   _____

   _____

Ongoing Review

3. On how many tests did Anna score more than 83?

   A. 1   **B.** 3   **C.** 6   **D.** 7

Counting Around the Class

In these counting problems, each student said
one number.

NOTE Students use their
knowledge of multiples to
solve these related problems.

SMH 25

1. The students in Ms. Alonzo's class counted by 5s.
   The first student said 5, the second student said 10,
   and the third said 15. How many students

   counted to get to 250? _____
   How do you know?

2. The students in Mr. Nelson's class counted by 10s.
   The first student said 10, the second student said 20,
   and the third said 30. How many students counted

   to get to 250? _____
   How do you know?

3. **a.** The students in Ms. Weinberg's class counted by
   25s. The first student said 25, the second student
   said 50, and the third student said 75. How many

   students counted to get to 250? _____
   How do you know?

   b. When the students in Ms. Weinberg's class counted
   by 25s, did anyone say 200? _____
   How do you know?

Record of Cubes in a Bag

1. Record how many of each color cube are in your bag.

   _____ red cubes   _____ blue cubes

2. Prediction: How many times do you think you will pull a red cube out of the bag?

3. Record which color you pull out on each trial.

4. Total number of red cubes: _____

Arranging Cans of Juice

> **NOTE** Students find factors by arranging numbers into rectangular arrays.
>
> **SMH** 23

1. a. You have 32 cans of juice. Show all the ways you can arrange these cans into arrays. Draw the arrays in the space below.

2. a. Mauricio has 36 cans of juice. Show all the ways he can arrange his cans into arrays. Draw the arrays in the space below.

b. List all the factors of 32.

b. List all the factors of 36.

Ongoing Review

3. Which number is prime?

    A. 49   **B.** 27   **C.** 17   **D.** 9

Comparing Probability Experiments (page 1 of 2)

Experiment 1: 10 red cubes and 10 blue cubes

1. How many red cubes did you draw in 50 trials? _____

2. Did the number you got surprise you, or is it about what you expected? Why?

   _____

   _____

3. Look at the class line plot. What do you notice about the data for Experiment 1?

   _____

   _____

Experiment 2: 5 red cubes and 15 blue cubes

4. How many red cubes did you draw in 50 trials? _____

5. Did the number you got surprise you, or is it about what you expected? Why?

   _____

   _____

6. Look at the class line plot. What do you notice about the data for Experiment 2?

   _____

   _____

   _____

   _____

Comparing Probability Experiments (page 2 of 2)

Experiment 3: 15 red cubes and 5 blue cubes

7. How many red cubes did you draw in 50 trials? _____

8. Did the number you got surprise you, or is it about what you expected? Why?

_____

_____

9. Look at the class line plot. What do you notice about the data for Experiment 3?

_____

_____

10. What do you notice when you compare the results from the three experiments?

_____

_____

_____

_____

Leg Riddles

NOTE Students solve multiplication and division problems in story problem contexts.

Birds have 2 legs.
Dogs have 4 legs.
Ladybugs have 6 legs.

1. There are 48 legs, and they all belong to dogs. How many dogs are there?

2. There are 3 ladybugs, 7 dogs, and 13 birds in the house. How many legs are there altogether?

3. There are 36 legs in the house. All the legs belong to birds, dogs, and ladybugs. How many of each creature—birds, dogs, and ladybugs—might be in the house?

(There are many possible answers. How many can you find?)

Birds	Dogs	Ladybugs

Don't Miss The Bus!

Josh takes the bus to school every day. The bus is supposed to arrive at his stop at 7:30. For one month, Josh notes the times that the bus arrives in the morning. The table shows the data he collected.

NOTE Students solve real-world problems involving the math content of this unit.

SMH 88–91

7:30	7:28	7:31	7:29	7:36
7:40	7:31	7:28	7:35	7:31
7:36	7:33	7:35	7:29	7:31
7:34	7:36	7:29	7:33	7:30

1. Make a line plot of the data Josh collected. Remember to label your line plot.

2. What time will the bus most likely arrive? Why do you think so?

3. What time does Josh need to be at the bus stop to make sure he does not miss the bus? Use the data from the line plot to explain your thinking.

© Pearson Education 4

Investigations

IN NUMBER, DATA, AND SPACE®

Multiple Towers and Division Stories

Mr. Jones and the Bagels

Solve these story problems. Show your thinking.

1. Mr. Jones needs to buy 14 dozen bagels for a big party. How many bagels does he need to buy? (Remember that a dozen is 12.)

2. Mr. Jones goes to the bagel shop. They have only 10 dozen left! So he buys them all. How many bagels does he buy at the bagel shop?

3. Mr. Jones goes to the supermarket to buy the rest of the bagels. How many more bagels does Mr. Jones need to buy? How do you know?

4. What if the bagel shop had only 7 dozen bagels left? How many bagels would Mr. Jones have to buy at the supermarket then?

Multiplication Story Problems

Solve these story problems. Show your thinking.

1. Ruth and Manuel are helping Mr. Jones set up for the party. They will need 8 chairs at each table. Ruth sets up 9 tables, and Manuel sets up 9 tables. How many chairs do they need altogether?

2. Mr. Jones bought cans of juice, which come in 6-packs. He bought twelve 6-packs of orange juice and three 6-packs of apple juice. How many cans of juice did he buy?

3. Mr. Jones realizes that he didn't buy enough juice! He goes back to the store and finds juice boxes that come in 9-packs. He buys ten 9-packs of orange juice and six 9-packs of apple juice. How many juice boxes does he buy?

Planning a Party

Solve these story problems. Show your thinking.

> **NOTE** Students practice solving multiplication problems in a story context.

1. Ms. Ruiz bought 15 packages of cups for a big party. Each package contains 8 cups. How many cups did she buy?

2. Ms. Ruiz bought 9 packages of plates for the party. Each package contains 14 plates. How many plates did she buy?

3. Ms. Ruiz bought 8 packages of napkins for the party. Each package contains 16 napkins. How many napkins did she buy?

Ongoing Review

4. Which of these has a product less than 60?

   A. 7×9 **B.** 6×12 **C.** 5×11 **D.** 8×8

Practice with Multiplication Cards 1

NOTE Students are working on the multiplication combinations (facts) to 12 × 12. Help your child with this practice.

SMH 29–34

1. Which multiplication combinations are you practicing?

_____

_____

_____

2. Write two multiplication combinations that are hard for you, and explain what helps you remember them.

Multiplication combination: _____

What helps me: _____

_____

_____

Multiplication combination: _____

What helps me: _____

_____

_____

3. How did you practice your multiplication combinations? Who helped you?

_____

_____

_____

Related Multiplication Combinations

Solve these problems.

NOTE Students practice multiplication combinations (facts) in related sets.

SMH 29–34

1. $5 \times 9 =$ _____ $10 \times 9 =$ _____	**2.** $4 \times 6 =$ _____ $8 \times 6 =$ _____	**3.** $11 \times 4 =$ _____ $11 \times 8 =$ _____
4. $7 \times 5 =$ _____ $7 \times 7 =$ _____ $7 \times 12 =$ _____	**5.** $4 \times 9 =$ _____ $8 \times 9 =$ _____ $12 \times 9 =$ _____	**6.** $8 \times 3 =$ _____ $8 \times 6 =$ _____ $8 \times 12 =$ _____
7. $2 \times 2 =$ _____ $4 \times 4 =$ _____ $8 \times 8 =$ _____	**8.** $7 \times 6 =$ _____ $7 \times 8 =$ _____ $7 \times 10 =$ _____	**9.** $3 \times 11 =$ _____ $6 \times 11 =$ _____ $12 \times 11 =$ _____
10. $9 \times 3 =$ _____ $9 \times 6 =$ _____ $9 \times 9 =$ _____	**11.** $6 \times 3 =$ _____ $6 \times 6 =$ _____ $6 \times 12 =$ _____	**12.** $12 \times 5 =$ _____ $10 \times 5 =$ _____ $8 \times 5 =$ _____

Tickets for the Play

Solve these story problems. Use
equations to show your thinking.

NOTE Students are working on
breaking multiplication problems apart
to make them easier to solve. Here,
they practice solving multiplication
problems in a story context.

SMH **40**

1. The fourth grade is going to see a
   play. The tickets cost $8 each. There
   are 22 students in the class. How much
   do the tickets for the whole class cost?

2. By Wednesday, half of the class had brought in their
   ticket money. How much money did the class have
   so far?

3. No one brought in any ticket money on Thursday.
   On Friday, 10 students brought in their ticket money.
   How much money was collected on Friday?

4. Had the class collected all the money that they needed
   for the play by Friday? Explain how you know whether
   they have all the money.

© Pearson Education 4

Small Array/Big Array Recording Sheet

Record each match you make with two equations, as in the example. Use parentheses to show the small arrays that make up the big array.

Example:

3 × 11 11 × 3
2 × 11 11 × 2

Equation: 5 × 11 = (3 × 11) + (2 × 11)
          55   =   33   +   22

1.	
2.	
3.	
4.	
5.	
6.	
7.	
8.	
9.	
10.	

© Pearson Education 4

Matching Arrays

Complete the multiplication equation illustrated
by each set of arrays.

NOTE Students practice breaking
multiplication problems apart to
make them easier to solve.

SMH 19

1.

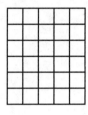

$6 \times 5 = (\underline{\hspace{1cm}} \times 5) + (\underline{\hspace{1cm}} \times 5)$

2.

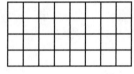 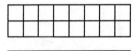

$4 \times \underline{\hspace{1cm}} = (\underline{\hspace{1cm}} \times \underline{\hspace{1cm}}) + (\underline{\hspace{1cm}} \times \underline{\hspace{1cm}})$

3.

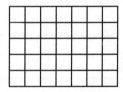 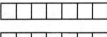 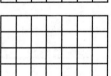

$\underline{\hspace{1cm}} \times \underline{\hspace{1cm}} = (\underline{\hspace{1cm}} \times \underline{\hspace{1cm}}) + (\underline{\hspace{1cm}} \times \underline{\hspace{1cm}})$

4. Draw an array of your own choosing. Then draw two
more arrays that together match your first array. Write
a multiplication equation for your diagram.

Factors and Products 1

Fill in the chart with the missing factors or products.

NOTE Students continue to practice multiplication combinations (facts) for fluency. They find a factor or product in some of the more difficult combinations.

SMH **40**

Factor	×	Factor	=	Product
12	×	9	=	
	×	7	=	63
11	×	8	=	
9	×		=	54
8	×	8	=	
	×	6	=	48
5	×	9	=	
6	×		=	60
4	×		=	28

Breaking Up Arrays

1. Two small arrays have been combined to make a big array. What are the dimensions and product of the big array? Fill in the equation that shows this big array broken into two small arrays.

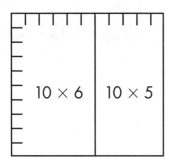   

Big Array

Dimensions of the big array: _____

Product: _____

Equation: _____ × _____ = (_____ × _____) + (_____ × _____)

2. Draw an array for 12 × 7. (You don't have to draw all the boxes inside, just the shape and the dimensions.) How would you break up this array into two smaller arrays? Show your two smaller arrays on your drawing. Then fill in the equation and solve the problem.

Array:

Equation: _____ × _____ = (_____ × _____) + (_____ × _____)
Product: 12 × 7 = _____

Solving Multiplication Problems (page 1 of 2)

Solve these problems. Show your thinking.

1. How many wheels are on 27 cars?

2. How many arms are on 21 starfish?

3. How many days are in 16 weeks?

JANUARY						
S	M	T	W	T	F	S
1	2	3	4	5	6	7

Solving Multiplication Problems (page 2 of 2)

Solve these problems. Show your thinking.

4. 5 × 19 =

5. 23 × 3 =

6. 6 × 13 =

Find the Missing Factors

Fill in the missing factors in each problem.

NOTE Students practice multiplication combinations (facts) in related sets.

 29–34

1.

$8 \times$ _____ $= 40$

$8 \times$ _____ $= 80$

2.

$3 \times$ _____ $= 9$

$3 \times$ _____ $= 18$

3.

$5 \times$ _____ $= 15$

$5 \times$ _____ $= 30$

$5 \times$ _____ $= 45$

4.

_____ $\times 4 = 16$

_____ $\times 6 = 36$

5.

$6 \times$ _____ $= 24$

$12 \times$ _____ $= 24$

6.

_____ $\times 7 = 42$

_____ $\times 7 = 84$

7.

$10 \times$ _____ $= 60$

$12 \times$ _____ $= 60$

8.

_____ $\times 6 = 36$

_____ $\times 6 = 72$

9.

_____ $\times 3 = 18$

_____ $\times 3 = 36$

10.

_____ $\times 2 = 14$

_____ $\times 4 = 28$

_____ $\times 8 = 56$

11.

$4 \times$ _____ $= 48$

$6 \times$ _____ $= 48$

$12 \times$ _____ $= 48$

12.

_____ $\times 12 = 144$

_____ $\times 6 = 72$

_____ $\times 3 = 36$

Multiple Towers and Division Stories

Lots of Legs

Solve these problems. Show your thinking.

NOTE Students practice solving multiplication problems.

SMH 16–17

1. How many legs are on 21 spiders?

2. How many legs are on 28 horses?

3. $5 \times 17 =$

4. $24 \times 6 =$

Ongoing Review

5. Which product does **not** equal 100?

   A. 50×2 **B.** 4×20 **C.** 10×10 **D.** 25×4

Division Stories (page 1 of 2)

Solve these problems. You may use cubes, grid paper, drawings, or other math tools to help you. Show how you solved each problem.

1. The 48 fourth graders at the Glendale School are taking a field trip to the science museum. They need to split into groups of 3 students for a special science project at the museum. How many groups will there be?

2. At the science museum gift shop, Michelle, Devon, Teresa, and Omar buy a bag of 64 marbles. They want to divide the marbles equally among the 4 of them. How many marbles will each fourth grader get?

Division Stories (page 2 of 2)

3. Ms. Santos got a shipment of 84 oranges. She has room for 6 rows of oranges on a table in her window display. How many oranges will be in each row if she puts the same number in each row?

4. Ms. Santos asks her helper to divide a box of 65 apples into bags of 5 apples each. How many bags can her helper make?

Multiplication Combinations of 2s, 4s, and 8s

NOTE Students practice multiplication combinations (facts). They look for patterns in the 2s, 4s, and 8s combinations.

SMH 29–34

1. Solve these problems.

   $1 \times 2 =$

   $2 \times 2 =$ $1 \times 4 =$

   $3 \times 2 =$

   $4 \times 2 =$ $2 \times 4 =$ $1 \times 8 =$

   $5 \times 2 =$

   $6 \times 2 =$ $3 \times 4 =$

   $7 \times 2 =$

   $8 \times 2 =$ $4 \times 4 =$ $2 \times 8 =$

   $9 \times 2 =$

   $10 \times 2 =$ $5 \times 4 =$

   $11 \times 2 =$

   $12 \times 2 =$ $6 \times 4 =$ $3 \times 8 =$

2. What pattern do you notice?

Practice with Multiplication Cards 2

NOTE Students are working on the multiplication combinations (facts) to 12 × 12. Help your child with this practice.

SMH 33–34

1. Which multiplication combinations are you practicing?

_____

_____

_____

2. Write two multiplication combinations that are hard for you, and explain what helps you remember them.

Multiplication combination: _____

What helps me: _____

_____

_____

Multiplication combination: _____

What helps me: _____

_____

_____

3. How did you practice your multiplication combinations? Who helped you?

_____

_____

_____

What Do You Do with the Extras? (page 1 of 2)

Solve the division problem. Then solve each story problem. You may use cubes or drawings to help you. For each problem, decide what to do with the extras. Be sure to show your work.

44 ÷ 8 = _____

1. There are 44 people taking a trip in some small vans. Each van holds 8 people. How many vans will they need?

2. If 8 people share 44 crackers equally, how many crackers does each person get?

Story Problems 1

Solve each problem. Show your work. Write a multiplication or division equation for each one.

NOTE Students practice solving multiplication and division problems in a story problem context.

 16, 44

1. Becca is building toy cars. She bought a box of 60 little wheels to use on the cars. How many cars can she build with the 60 wheels?

2. On Monday, Ms. Wu bought 8 packages of pencils. Each package contains 6 pencils. On Tuesday, Ms. Wu went back to the store and bought 4 more packages. How many pencils did Ms. Wu buy in all?

More Division Stories (page 1 of 2)

Solve these problems. You may use cubes, grid paper, or other math tools. Keep track of all the steps you take. Write equations to show the steps of your solution.

1. Cheyenne and her father baked 72 cookies for the school bake sale. They plan to put them in bags of 4 cookies each. How many bags of cookies can they fill?

   Division equation: _____72_____ ÷ _____4_____ = _____

   Answer: _____

2. Aliya, Ethan, Brianna, and Will saved up a total of $74 from returning bottles and cans. They want to share it equally among the 4 of them. How much money will each of the friends receive?

   Division equation: _____ ÷ _____ = _____

   Answer: _____

More Division Stories (page 2 of 2)

3. Juice boxes come in packages of 3. The fourth graders at Glendale School need 125 juice boxes for their field trip. How many packages of juice boxes will they have to buy?

   Division equation: _____ ÷ _____ = _____

   Answer: _____

4. The art teacher at Center School bought a box of 80 pencils for the 6 students in her drawing class. How many pencils will each student get if they share the pencils equally?

   Division equation: _____ ÷ _____ = _____

   Answer: _____

5. Ms. Washington's class counted around the class by 5s. Each student said one number. The number they ended on was 115. How many students counted?

   Division equation: _____ ÷ _____ = _____

   Answer: _____

Factor Pairs

For each of these numbers, list as many pairs of factors as you can.

NOTE Students practice multiplication combinations (facts) by finding pairs of factors for a given product.

SMH **23**

1. 36 Example: 3 × 12	**2.** 30
3. 40	**4.** 48
5. 60	**6.** 72

Ongoing Review

7. Which of these has the greatest product?

    A. 8 × 7   **B.** 9 × 6   **C.** 10 × 5   **D.** 11 × 4

Division and Remainders

Solve these problems. Write a division equation for each one.

> **NOTE** Students practice doing division and interpreting remainders in story problem contexts.
>
> SMH **47-49**

1. There are 70 people in line for the roller coaster. Each car holds 8 people. How many cars will it take for everyone to ride at the same time?

Division equation: _____ ÷ _____ = _____

Answer: _____

2. Eighty people bought tickets for a boat ride. Twelve people can ride in one boat. How many boats can be completely filled?

Division equation: _____ ÷ _____ = _____

Answer: _____

3. How many prizes could you get with 100 tickets?

Division equation:

_____ ÷ _____ = _____

Answer: _____

> **ARCADE PRIZES**
>
> **6 tickets per prize**

4. Mr. Brown's class counted around the class by 5s. The number they ended with was 135. How many students counted?

Division equation: _____ ÷ _____ = _____

Answer: _____

Ongoing Review

5. Ms. Gold's class counted around the class by 4s. There are 29 students in her class. Which of these numbers would NOT be said?

A. 54   **B.** 100   **C.** 76   **D.** 64

© Pearson Education 4

What's the Story? ✏️ WRITING

Write a story for each division problem.
Then solve them.

NOTE Students practice writing and solving division problems.

SMH **46**

1. $45 \div 9$

2. $84 \div 7$

Related Multiplication and Division Problems (page 1 of 2)

Solve the problems. Write a multiplication or division equation for each problem.

1. **a.** Ms. Santos got a new shipment of apples. There were 20 bags of apples in the shipment. Each bag contained 8 apples. How many apples did Ms. Santos receive?

   b. Jeff bought a book with 160 pages. If he reads 8 pages each day, how many days will it take him to finish the book?

   c. Did your solution to Problem 1a help you solve Problem 1b? If so, how?

Related Multiplication and Division Problems (page 2 of 2)

2. **a.** There are 3 fourth-grade classes at the Washington Elementary School. There are 21 students in each class. How many fourth graders are there in all?

b. Jessica and two of her friends earned $63 at a neighborhood car wash. They want to share the money equally among the 3 of them. How much money does each friend get?

c. Did your solution to Problem 2a help you solve Problem 2b? If so, how?

Factors and Products 2

NOTE Students practice solving multiplication problems.

Fill in the chart with the missing factors or products.

Factor	×	Factor	=	Product
10	×	5	=	
10	×		=	150
	×	20	=	100
	×	20	=	200
	×	20	=	300
25	×		=	75
25	×		=	150
25	×		=	300
4	×	25	=	
4	×		=	200
4	×		=	400
	×	10	=	200
	×	20	=	200
	×	25	=	200

Simpler Parts

Solve each problem by following the clues.

NOTE Students practice breaking division problems apart into smaller problems.

SMH 50–52

1. **136 ÷ 4 =** _____

   How many 4s are in 100? _____

   How many 4s are in 36? _____

   How many 4s are in 136? _____

2. **104 ÷ 8 =** _____

   How many 8s are in 80? _____

   How many 8s are in 24? _____

   How many 8s are in 104? _____

3. **162 ÷ 6 =** _____

   How many 6s are in 120? _____

   How many 6s are in 42? _____

   How many 6s are in 162? _____

Ongoing Review

4. Which of these expressions is equal to 6?

   A. 100 ÷ 20   **B.** 48 ÷ 8   **C.** 63 ÷ 9   **D.** 30 ÷ 3

About Our Multiple Tower (page 1 of 2)

Answer these questions about the multiple tower that you
and your partner built.

1. What number did you use to build your multiple tower? _____

2. What is the ending multiple on your tower? _____

3. How many multiples are in your tower? _____

4. What is one way to figure out how many multiples
   are in your tower without counting each one?

5. Write a multiplication equation that represents how
   many multiples are in your multiple tower.

   _____ × _____ = _____

About Our Multiple Tower (page 2 of 2)

Answer these next questions without counting.

6. What is the 10th multiple? _____

7. What is the 20th multiple? _____

8. What is the 25th multiple? _____

9. How did you decide what the 20th multiple is?

10. Find each of the multiples above (10th, 20th, 25th) on your tower, and label them with a multiplication expression, such as 10×30.

11. What other landmark multiples can you find and label?

Arranging Juice Cans

NOTE Students solve story problems that involve finding factors.

SMH **22**

1. You have 24 juice cans. Show all of the ways you can arrange these cans into arrays. Draw the arrays.

2. List all the factors of 24.

3. Teyo has 25 juice cans. Show all of the ways he can arrange his cans into arrays. Draw the arrays.

4. List all the factors of 25.

5. Karina says, "25 has more factors than 24 because 25 is greater than 24." Do you agree or disagree with Karina? Explain.

Multiple Towers and Division Stories   Homework

Practice with Multiplication Cards 3

NOTE Students are working on the multiplication combinations (facts) to 12×12. Help your child with this practice.

SMH 33–34

1. Which multiplication combinations are you practicing?

   _____

   _____

   _____

2. Write two multiplication combinations that are hard for you, and explain what helps you remember them.

   Multiplication combination: _____

   What helps me: _____

   _____

   _____

   Multiplication combination: _____

   What helps me: _____

   _____

   _____

3. How did you practice your multiplication combinations? Who helped you?

   _____

   _____

   _____

Problems About Oranges

Solve each problem. Record your solution with an
equation. Also, make a quick picture or diagram.

1. Ms. Santos sells bags of oranges in her grocery store.
   There are 4 oranges in each bag. David bought 6 bags
   of oranges to bring to his class. How many oranges did
   David buy?

2. When Ms. Santos orders oranges from the fruit company,
   they come in boxes. Each box has 40 oranges inside.
   Last week, Ms. Santos ordered 6 boxes of oranges.
   How many oranges did she order?

Multiplying by Multiples of 10: What Happens? (page 1 of 2)

Solve these problems.

1.

$5 \times 6 =$

$50 \times 6 =$

$5 \times 60 =$

2.

$3 \times 4 =$

$30 \times 4 =$

$3 \times 40 =$

3.

$8 \times 6 =$

$80 \times 6 =$

$8 \times 60 =$

Multiplying by Multiples of 10: What Happens? (page 2 of 2)

Now answer the following questions.

4. What do you notice about your solutions to the problems on page 42? In each set, how are your answers related?

5. Choose one of the sets of problems from page 42, and use cubes or a picture or diagram to show your thinking.

6. Try solving this problem:
$3 \times 400 =$

How is your answer to this problem different from your answer to 3×40? Why do you think that is?

Multiple Towers and Division Stories

Kayla's Multiple Tower

The picture shows part of Kayla's
multiple tower.

> **NOTE** Students practice solving
> multiplication and division problems.
>
> **SMH** 36

1. What number did Kayla count by?
   How do you know?

2. How many numbers are in Kayla's tower so far?
   How do you know?

3. Write a multiplication equation that represents
   how many numbers are in Kayla's multiple tower.

   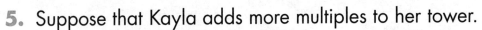

   _____ × _____ = _____

216
198
180
162
144

4. What is the 10th multiple in Kayla's tower?

5. Suppose that Kayla adds more multiples to her tower.
   a. What would be the 20th multiple in her tower?
   How do you know?

   b. What would be the 25th multiple in her tower?
   How do you know?

Ongoing Review

6. Which of these numbers is not on Kayla's
   multiple tower?

   A. 9   **B.** 18   **C.** 72   **D.** 90

Story Problems 2 (page 1 of 2)

Solve the story problem. Show your solution with equations. You may also show your solutions with arrays or pictures of groups.

NOTE Students practice multiplying by a number that is a multiple of 10 in a story problem context.

SMH 37–38

1. Ms. O'Riley, the art teacher, orders crayons that come in boxes of 40. This year she ordered 9 boxes. How many crayons did she order?

Story Problems 2 (page 2 of 2)

2. Write a story problem to go with the following multiplication expression. Then solve the problem and show your thinking.

$7 \times 50 =$

Multiples of 10: Related Problems

Solve each pair of multiplication problems.

1.

3 × 9 = _____

90 × 3 = _____

2.

8 × 7 = _____

8 × 70 = _____

3.

6 × 6 = _____

6 × 60 = _____

4.

2 × 12 = _____

20 × 12 = _____

5.

15 × 2 = _____

150 × 2 = _____

6.

4 × 10 = _____

10 × 40 = _____

7. Choose one of these problem pairs.
Write a story problem to go with it.

_____

_____

_____

_____

_____

_____

Story Problems About 10s

Solve these problems. Show your solutions with equations.
You may also use arrays or pictures.

1. Last month Lakewood School ordered 8 boxes of
    erasers with 20 erasers in each box. How many
    erasers did they order?

2. Every year, Ms. Ortega orders a box of 50 erasers
    for each classroom at Riverview School. There are
    11 classrooms in the school. How many erasers
    does Ms. Ortega order?

3. Last year at Lincoln School, Mr. Johnson ordered
    7 boxes each with 120 erasers. How many erasers
    did Mr. Johnson order?

Things That Come in Groups

Solve these problems. Write a multiplication equation
for each problem. Show how you solved it.

NOTE Students practice
multiplication by solving
story problems.

SMH **16, 17**

Spiders have 8 legs.

1. How many legs do 6 spiders have? _____

   Equation: _____

2. How many legs do 12 spiders have? _____

   Equation: _____

3. How many legs do 18 spiders have? _____

   Equation: _____

Multiplying Groups of 10

Solve each pair of multiplication problems.

NOTE Students are learning how multiplying one number in a multiplication problem by 10 affects the product. Here, they solve problems with numbers that are multiples of 10.

SMH 38

1.

$8 \times 4 =$ _____

$8 \times 40 =$ _____

2.

$6 \times 7 =$ _____

$6 \times 70 =$ _____

3.

$9 \times 5 =$ _____

$90 \times 5 =$ _____

4.

$12 \times 6 =$ _____

$120 \times 6 =$ _____

5.

$15 \times 4 =$ _____

$15 \times 40 =$ _____

6.

$5 \times 14 =$ _____

$50 \times 14 =$ _____

7.

$11 \times 3 =$ _____

$11 \times 30 =$ _____

8.

$40 \times 5 =$ _____

$400 \times 5 =$ _____

More Things That Come in Groups

NOTE Students practice multiplication by solving story problems.

SMH **16, 17**

Solve these problems. Write a multiplication equation for each problem. Show how you solved it.

A package has 9 frozen juice bars.

1. How many frozen juice bars are in 3 packages? _____

   Equation: _____

2. How many frozen juice bars are in 6 packages? _____

   Equation: _____

3. How many frozen juice bars are in 12 packages? _____

   Equation: _____

Ms. Santos's Apples

Solve these problems. Record your solution with equations. Use pictures or diagrams to show what is happening in the problem.

1. Ms. Santos has 168 apples. She wants to pack them into boxes with 28 in each box. How many boxes does she need?

2. When Ms. Santos started to pack the apples into boxes, she found that her boxes were too small. She could fit only 14 apples in each box. Now how many boxes does she need?

Doubles and Halves (page 1 of 2)

1. Solve the first problem in each pair. Can you use the
   first problem to help you solve the second problem?

a.	**b.**	**c.**
$8 \times 4 =$ _____	$8 \times 6 =$ _____	$16 \times 3 =$ _____
$16 \times 4 =$ _____	$16 \times 3 =$ _____	$16 \times 6 =$ _____
d.	**e.**	**f.**
$9 \times 8 =$ _____	$18 \times 8 =$ _____	$15 \times 8 =$ _____
$18 \times 4 =$ _____	$18 \times 4 =$ _____	$30 \times 4 =$ _____

2. Choose one pair of equations from **1a, 1c,** or **1e.**

   a. Use arrays, pictures, cubes, or a story context to
   show both problems in the pair.

   b. What is different about each problem in this pair?
   What is the same? How does the first problem help
   you solve the second problem?

   _____

   _____

   _____

   _____

   _____

   _____

Doubles and Halves (page 2 of 2)

3. Choose one pair of equations from **1b, 1d,** or **1f.**

   a. Use arrays, pictures, cubes, or a story context to show both problems in the pair.

   b. What is different about each problem in this pair? What is the same? How does the first problem help you solve the second problem?

_____

_____

_____

_____

_____

_____

_____

Counting Around the Class 1

Solve these problems.

NOTE Students find the multiples of a given number and solve multiplication problems.

SMH 25

1. Mr. Bugwadia's class counted by 10s. Each person said one number. The first person said 10, the second said 20, and the third said 30.

   How many people counted to get to 200? _____
   How do you know?

2. Ms. Tan's class counted by 20s. Each person said one number. The first person said 20, the second said 40, and the third said 60.

   a. How many people counted to get to 420? _____
   How do you know?

   b. When Ms. Tan's class counted by 20s, did anyone say the number 300? _____
   How do you know?

Division Practice

Solve the problems. Use equations to show your thinking. You may also use arrays or pictures of groups.

NOTE Students practice solving division problems both with and without story contexts.

SMH 46

1. A case of apple juice holds 78 cans. How many 6-packs of apple juice can the case hold?

2. Mr. Yamada's class has 18 students. If the class counts around by a number and ends with 90, what number did they count by?

3. $7\overline{)79}$

4. $112 \div 20 =$ _____

5. There are 114 students in all of the fourth-grade classes combined. For Field Day, they need to make 9 teams. How many students will be on each team?

Multiplication Cluster Problems (page 1 of 2)

Solve the first three or four problems in each cluster. Then
solve the final problem, using one or more of the cluster
problems (along with other problems if you need them).
Show your strategy for solving the final problem.

Set A Solve these problems. How did you solve the final problem?

$4 \times 10 =$

$4 \times 40 =$

$4 \times 3 =$

$2 \times 43 =$

Final problem: **$4 \times 43 =$**

Set B Solve these problems. How did you solve the final problem?

$5 \times 6 =$

$50 \times 6 =$

$58 \times 2 =$

Final problem: **$58 \times 6 =$**

Set C Solve these problems. How did you solve the final problem?

$32 \times 2 =$

$10 \times 8 =$

$30 \times 8 =$

Final problem: **$32 \times 8 =$**

Multiplication Cluster Problems (page 2 of 2)

Solve the first three or four problems in each cluster. Then solve the final problem, using one or more of the cluster problems (along with other problems if you need them). Show your strategy for solving the final problem.

Set D Solve these problems. How did you solve the final problem?

$63 \times 10 =$

$60 \times 11 =$

$3 \times 11 =$

Final problem: $\mathbf{63 \times 11 =}$

Set E Solve these problems. How did you solve the final problem?

$5 \times 12 =$

$10 \times 12 =$

$25 \times 6 =$

$50 \times 6 =$

Final problem: $\mathbf{25 \times 12 =}$

Set F Solve these problems. How did you solve the final problem?

$76 \times 10 =$

$70 \times 5 =$

$6 \times 5 =$

Final problem: $\mathbf{76 \times 5 =}$

Multiplication Pairs

Solve each pair of multiplication problems below.
Can you use the first problem to help you solve
the second problem?

NOTE Students practice solving related multiplication problems.

1. $12 \times 7 =$ _____ $24 \times 7 =$ _____	**2.** $15 \times 8 =$ _____ $30 \times 4 =$ _____
3. $25 \times 4 =$ _____ $25 \times 8 =$ _____	**4.** $9 \times 7 =$ _____ $18 \times 7 =$ _____
5. $28 \times 5 =$ _____ $14 \times 10 =$ _____	**6.** $9 \times 6 =$ _____ $19 \times 6 =$ _____

Ongoing Review

7. Which of the following does not equal 12×8?

     A. 24×4 **B.** 2×48 **C.** 3×28 **D.** 6×16

© Pearson Education 4

Multiple Towers and Division Stories   Homework

Factors and Products 3

Fill in the chart with the missing factors or products.

Can you solve some of these mentally?

NOTE Students practice multiplying and dividing.

SMH 35

Factor	×	Factor	=	Product
2	×	54	=	
4	×	27	=	
6	×		=	120
5	×		=	125
3	×	16	=	
7	×		=	84
8	×	60	=	
10	×		=	150
9	×	21	=	

More Multiplication Problems (page 1 of 2)

Solve these problems. Show your solutions with equations.

1. A yard has 36 inches. How many inches are in
   8 yards?

2. A lunar month is 28 days. How many days are in
   5 lunar months?

3. A year has 52 weeks. How many weeks are in
   4 years?

More Multiplication Problems (page 2 of 2)

Solve these problems. Show your solutions with equations.

4. $16 \times 4 =$

5. $24 \times 7 =$

6. $30 \times 16 =$

7. $47 \times 3 =$

8. $23 \times 12 =$

9. Choose one of the problems above and solve it a second way, using a different strategy than the one you used the first time.

Counting Around the Class 2

NOTE Students find the multiples of a given number and solve multiplication problems.

SMH 25

1. Ms. Garcia's class counted by 25s. The first person said 25, the second person said 50, and the third said 75.

   How many people counted to get to 400? _____
   How do you know?

2. Mr. Wilson's class counted by 20s. The first person said 20, the second person said 40, and the third said 60.

   How many people counted to get to 400? _____
   How do you know?

3. Ms. Kleinman's class counted by 40s. The first person said 40, the second person said 80, and the third person said 120.

   a. How many people counted to get to 400? _____
   How do you know?

   b. When Ms. Kleinman's class counted by 40s, did anyone say the number 300? _____
   How do you know?

Solving a Cluster Problem

NOTE Students practice solving clusters of familiar multiplication problems, which can help them solve a related problem with larger numbers.

SMH **39**

Solve the three multiplication cluster problems. Then solve the final problem. Explain how you solved the final problem, including which equations from the cluster helped you.

1. Cluster: $7 \times 3 =$

$7 \times 30 =$

$7 \times 4 =$

2. Final problem: **$7 \times 34 =$**

3. How did you solve 7×34?

Leg Riddles

People have 2 legs.
Cats have 4 legs.
Spiders have 8 legs.

NOTE Students solve multiplication problems in story problem contexts.

1. There are 3 spiders, 2 cats, and 5 people in the house. How many legs are there altogether?

2. There are 28 legs, and they all belong to cats. How many cats are there?

3. There are 30 legs in the house. All of the legs belong to people, cats, and spiders. How many of each creature—people, cats, and spiders—might be in the house?

   There are many possible answers. How many can you find?

People	Cats	Spiders

Sunken Treasure

Solve the problems. Use another sheet of paper if you need to. Show equations, pictures, and diagrams. Decide what to do with any extras.

NOTE Students solve division problems in a real-world context.

SMH **50–52**

1. These are gold coins found at the site of a shipwreck. If a scuba diver could carry 18 of these coins to the surface in one trip, how many trips would it take to carry 108 coins?

2. If a scuba diver could carry 36 coins to the surface in one trip, how many trips would it take to carry 108 coins?

3. If five scuba divers found a total of 108 coins and were allowed to share them equally, how many coins would each scuba diver get?

4. If the five scuba divers were allowed to share only half of the 108 coins, how many coins would they each get?

© Pearson Education 4

Polished Spiral Karin Kuhlmann

"Although the creation of fractals is bounded to strict mathematical rules, the results are always very inspiring." – **Karin Kuhlmann**

Investigations
IN NUMBER, DATA, AND SPACE®

Size, Shape, and Symmetry

© Pearson Education 4

Size, Shape, and Symmetry

Measurement Benchmarks

Use a ruler, a yardstick, and a meter stick to find objects that are about as long as these measurement units. Record what you find.

Centimeter	Inch	Foot
Example: the tip of my pencil		

Yard	Meter
	Example: the height of the wall from the floor to the board

Using Measurement Benchmarks and Measurement Tools

Object	Estimate	Actual Measurement
Length of my pencil		
Width of my pencil		
Height of my desk from the floor		
Length of my notebook		
Width of the classroom window		
My teacher's height		

Factors and Products

Fill in the chart below with the missing factors or products. Can you solve these mentally?

> **NOTE** Students practice multiplying and dividing multiples of 10.
>
> **SMH** 37–38

Factor	×	Factor	=	Product
1. 6	×	30	=	_____
2. 12	×	50	=	_____
3. 9	×	_____	=	270
4. 5	×	_____	=	300
5. 7	×	80	=	_____
6. 11	×	_____	=	220
7. 8	×	60	=	_____
8. 10	×	_____	=	340
9. 80	×	4	=	_____

Size, Shape, and Symmetry

When and How Do You Measure Length?

NOTE Students think about when measurement is used in the real world by adults.

SMH 101–102

Ask an adult to tell you about at least four situations in which he or she measures. Write each situation in one of the boxes. Answer the following questions about each situation.

- Did you need to measure exactly or estimate?
- If you estimated, how did you estimate?
- What tools did you use?

Situation 1:

Situation 2:

Situation 3:

Situation 4:

© Pearson Education 4

Multiplication Problems

Solve each of the problems below.
Show your thinking.

NOTE Students practice solving multiplication problems.

SMH 40, 41, 42

1. 22 × 6 = _____

2. 40 × 14 = _____

3. 4 × 29 = _____

4. 36 × 5 = _____

5. 8 × 26 = _____

6. 12 × 31 = _____

Size, Shape, and Symmetry

Homework

How Tall Is an Adult?

1. Measure the height of an adult outside of class and then record it. You can record it in feet and inches or in centimeters.

NOTE Students practice measuring at home by choosing any measurement tool that they have available.

SMH 101–103

2. Describe what tools you used and how you used the tools to measure the adult.

Size, Shape, and Symmetry

Perimeter Problems (page 1 of 2)

1. Estimate, and then find the perimeter of the objects listed below. Choose your own objects for the blank spaces.

Object	Unit of Measure (inches, feet, yards, centimeters, or meters)	Estimate	Actual Measurement
Your classroom door			
Your teacher's desk			
The board			

Perimeter Problems (page 2 of 2)

2. Choose one of your perimeter measurements.
   Estimate and measure it again using another unit.

3. Explain why the two measurements of the same
   perimeter are different.

What Should We Do with the Extras?

Solve the problems below. Make sure to keep
track of all the steps that you take. Write equations
to show the steps of your solution.

NOTE Students practice
solving division problems and
interpreting remainders in a
story problem context.

 48–49

1. Noemi is building toy cars. She bought a box of
   50 wheels to use on the cars. How many cars can
   she build with the 50 wheels? How many wheels
   will she have left?

   Division Equation: _____ ÷ _____ = _____   Answer: _____

2. Steve, Jill, Lucy, Ursula, and Terrell earned $106 by
   raking leaves. They want to share the money equally
   among the five of them. How much money will each of
   the friends receive?

   Division Equation: _____ ÷ _____ = _____   Answer: _____

3. Juice boxes come in packages of six. The fourth
   graders at the Glendale School need 82 juice boxes
   for their field trip to the art museum. How many
   packages of juice boxes will they have to buy?
   Explain your answer.

   Division Equation: _____ ÷ _____ = _____   Answer: _____

Measuring Ribbon

Solve each problem and explain how you did it.

NOTE Students review multiplication and division work in a measurement context.

SMH 45

1. Marisol is measuring one piece of ribbon. She will cut it into 17 pieces that are each 9 inches long. How many inches long will the whole piece be?

    How did you solve it?

2. Sabrina is also measuring a piece of ribbon. She needs 22 pieces that are each 13 inches long. How long will her piece of ribbon be?

3. Bill has a piece of ribbon that is 144 inches long. He needs pieces that are 12 inches long. How many pieces can he cut?

Size, Shape, and Symmetry

Mapping 100 Feet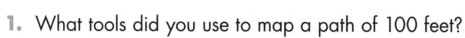

1. What tools did you use to map a path of 100 feet?

2. Draw your path.

3. What was the most challenging part of mapping out 100 feet?

Explaining Measurement Differences

1. Record all of the measurements your class found for the length of the classroom.

2. What is one of the smallest measurements? _____

3. Why did some people get smaller measurements?

4. What is one of the largest measurements? _____

5. Why did some people get larger measurements?

Handy Measure

If you spread out your hand, the length from your little finger to your thumb is your **hand span.** It is a handy measuring tool.

1. Use your hand span to measure four items. List the items and the length of each in spans.

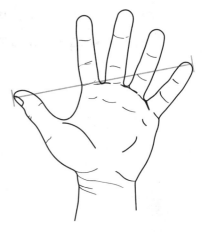

Item	Number of Spans

2. How can you estimate length in inches if you know the length of your hand span in inches?

Ongoing Review

3. Which of these units of measure would be best for measuring a raisin?

   A. foot   **B.** centimeter   **C.** meter   **D.** inch

Missing Measures

Imagine that each polygon below is the shape of a farmer's field. For each polygon, find the missing measure to complete the perimeter.

NOTE Students find the missing part of the perimeter of polygons.

SMH 104–105

1. The perimeter of this field is 702 yards.
The missing measure is _____.

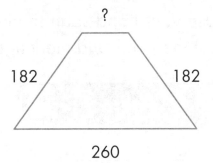

2. The perimeter of this field is 581 meters.
The missing measure is _____.

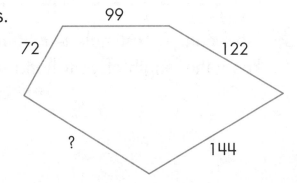

Ongoing Review

3. Which unit of measure below would be best for measuring the perimeter of your backyard?

A. centimeter   **B.** foot   **C.** inch   **D.** meter

© Pearson Education 4

Making Polygons (page 2 of 2)

Follow these directions to make new polygons from two or more Power Polygons. Trace each new polygon. Draw dotted lines to show the sides of the Power Polygons that you used and write the letter of each Power Polygon inside.

3. Make 2 different five-sided shapes.

4. Make 2 different six-sided shapes.

Names for Polygons

On the chart, write some words that have prefixes (like "tri" for triangle) that match the prefixes in the names for polygons. You do not have to fill in something for every polygon name.

Number of Sides	Name of Polygon	Words with the Same Prefix
3	Triangle	Example: triathlon (a race with 3 parts)
4	Quadrilateral	
5	Pentagon	
6	Hexagon	
7	Heptagon or Septagon	
8	Octagon	
9	Nonagon	
10	Decagon	
11	Hendecagon	
12	Dodecagon	

Division Stories

Write a division equation for each problem. Then, solve each problem and show your work.

NOTE Students practice solving division problems in a story problem context.

SMH 46

1. A case of juice holds 108 cans. How many six-packs of juice does the case hold?

2. Mrs. Santos has 112 oranges. She wants to pack them into bags with 8 oranges in each bag. How many bags does she need?

3. Mr. Harris's class counted around the class by 20s. The number they ended on was 400. How many students counted?

Sorting Polygons

Record at least 3 rules that you and your partner made for polygons when you played *Guess My Rule*. For each rule, write the numbers of the Shape Cards that fit the rule, and the numbers of 2 or 3 Shape Cards that did not fit the rule. (You may record more than 3 rules, or use this same sheet for another game.)

Rule	Polygons That Fit the Rule	Polygons That Do Not Fit the Rule

Making More Polygons (page 1 of 2)

Follow these directions to make new polygons from two
or more Power Polygons. Trace each new polygon. Draw
dotted lines to show the sides of the Power Polygons that
you used and write the letter of each Power Polygon inside.

1. Make two different shapes that have 7 sides.

2. Make two different shapes that have 8 sides.

Making More Polygons (page 2 of 2)

Follow these directions to make new polygons from two or more Power Polygons. Trace each new polygon. Draw dotted lines to show the sides of the Power Polygons that you used and write the letter of each Power Polygon inside.

3. Make two different shapes that have 9 sides.

4. Make two different shapes that have 10 sides.

Division Practice (page 1 of 2)

Solve each division problem below. Then write the related multiplication combination.

NOTE Students review division problems that are related to the multiplication combinations they know.

SMH 35

Division Problem	Multiplication Combination
1. $54 \div 6 =$ _____	_____ × _____ = _____
2. $77 \div 11 =$ _____	_____ × _____ = _____
3. $56 \div 7 =$ _____	_____ × _____ = _____
4. $108 \div 9 =$ _____	_____ × _____ = _____
5. $63 \div 7 =$ _____	_____ × _____ = _____

Division Practice (page 2 of 2)

Solve each division problem below. Then write the related multiplication combination.

Division Problem	Multiplication Combination
6. $81 \div 9 = $ _____	_____ × _____ = _____
7. $72 \div 8 = $ _____	_____ × _____ = _____
8. $144 \div 12 = $ _____	_____ × _____ = _____
9. $6\overline{)42}$	_____ × _____ = _____
10. $11\overline{)132}$	_____ × _____ = _____

Size, Shape, and Symmetry

All or Some Quadrilaterals

In these two columns, list attributes that are true for either all quadrilaterals or some quadrilaterals. Use the rules you made for *Guess My Rule* to help you.

All Quadrilaterals	Some Quadrilaterals

Can You Make These Polygons? (page 1 of 3)

Make new polygons from two or more Power Polygons that fit each of the descriptions below. Trace each new polygon. Draw dotted lines to show the sides of the Power Polygons that you used and write the letter of each Power Polygon inside. For each description, try to make as many different polygons as you can.

1. It is a quadrilateral. All of its sides are the same length.

2. It is a quadrilateral. All of its angles are the same size. Not all of its sides are the same length.

Can You Make These Polygons? (page 2 of 3)

Make new polygons from two or more Power Polygons that fit each of the descriptions below. Trace each new polygon. Draw dotted lines to show the sides of the Power Polygons that you used and write the letter of each Power Polygon inside. For each description, try to make as many different polygons as you can.

3. It is a quadrilateral. All of its sides are the same length. Not all of its angles are the same size.

4. It is a quadrilateral. All of its angles are the same size.

Can You Make These Polygons? (page 3 of 3)

Make new polygons from two or more Power
Polygons that fit each of the descriptions below.
Trace each new polygon. Draw dotted lines to show
the sides of the Power Polygons that you used and
write the letter of each Power Polygon inside. For
each description, try to make as many different
polygons as you can.

5. It is a triangle. All of its sides are the same length.

6. It is a triangle. All of its angles are different sizes.

Mystery Rectangles

NOTE Students consider the dimensions of various rectangles.

SMH 110

1. Draw a line from each Clue Card to the matching rectangle. One of the Clue Cards does not have a matching rectangle.

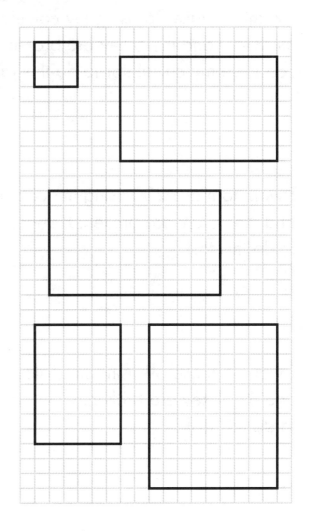

Clue Card 1
My length is twice as long as my width.

Clue Card 2
My length is 4 more than my width.

Clue Card 3
My perimeter is 28.

Clue Card 4
All my sides have the same length.

Clue Card 5
The sum of my length and width is a multiple of 10.

Ongoing Review

2. Which shapes are rectangles?

A. M and N   **C.** S and O

B. T and S   **D.** O and P

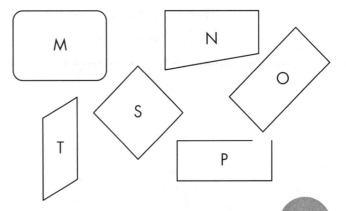

Today's Number: Broken Calculator

NOTE Students practice building flexibility with all operations (addition, subtraction, multiplication, and division).

Find five solutions to each of these problems.

1. I want to make 36 using my calculator, but the 3 key and the 6 key are broken. How can I use my calculator to do this task?

2. I want to make 200 using my calculator, but the 0 key and the + key are broken. How can I use my calculator to do this task?

3. I want to make 64 using my calculator, but the 6 key and the 4 key are broken. How can I use my calculator to do this task?

4. I want to make 55 using my calculator, but the 5 key, the + key, and the − key are broken. How can I use my calculator to do this task?

Sorting Quadrilaterals (page 1 of 2)

Write the numbers of all the quadrilaterals that belong in each category.

NOTE Students practice identifying properties in quadrilaterals.

 108–109

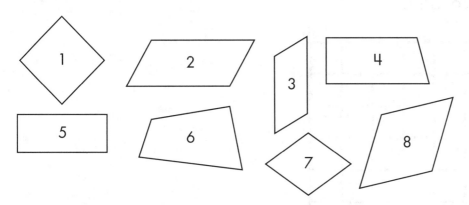

1. Which quadrilaterals have 4 right angles?

_____

_____

2. Which quadrilaterals have 2 pairs of parallel sides?

_____

_____

3. Which quadrilaterals have 4 sides of equal length?

_____

_____

Sorting Quadrilaterals (page 2 of 2)

Draw a shape to prove that each statement below is false.

4. All rectangles are squares.

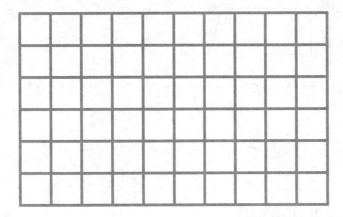

5. All quadrilaterals have at least one right angle.

Making Right Angles

Use the angles of two or more Power Polygons to make a
right angle. Trace the polygons that you used and label
each with its letter.

1.	**2.**
3.	**4.**
5.	**6.**

Which Angles Are Right Angles?

NOTE Students identify right angles (90 degree angles).

SMH 111–112

In each of the polygons below, there is at least one right angle. Find all of the right angles in each polygon and label them with an "R."

1.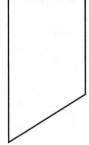

2.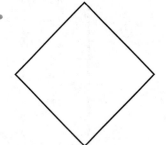

3.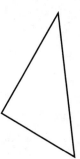

4.

5.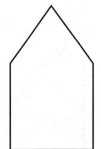

6.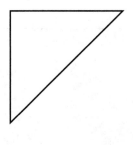

Ongoing Review

7. Suppose the arrow at the right is turned 90 degrees clockwise (right) three times. Which figure shows the new direction of the arrow?

A. 　　**B.** 　　**C.** 　　**D.**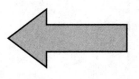

How Many Degrees? (page 1 of 2)

A right angle is measured as 90 degrees. How many degrees is each of these angles? Use Power Polygons to help you answer each question. Explain your thinking and include any drawings that will make your idea clear.

1. How many degrees is this angle? How do you know?

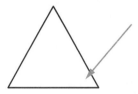

2. How many degrees is this angle? How do you know?

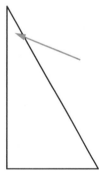

How Many Degrees? (page 2 of 2)

3. How many degrees is this angle? How do you know?

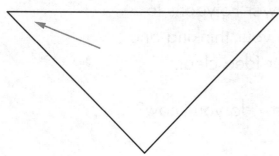

4. How many degrees is this angle? How do you know?

Building Angles (page 1 of 3)

Use the angles of two or more Power Polygons to make the angles described. Trace the polygons that you used and label them with their letters.

1. a. Make an angle that measures 60 degrees.

b. Explain how you know that this is a 60° angle.

c. Can you make a 60° angle in more than one way? Explain.

Building Angles (page 2 of 3)

Use the angles of two or more Power Polygons to make the angles described. Trace the polygons that you used and label them with their letters.

2. a. Make an angle that measures 120 degrees.

b. Explain how you know that this is a 120° angle.

c. Can you make a 120° angle in more than one way? Explain.

Building Angles (page 3 of 3)

Use the angles of two or more Power Polygons to make the angles described. Trace the polygons that you used and label them with their letters.

3. a. Make an angle that measures 150 degrees.

b. Explain how you know that this is a 150° angle.

c. Can you make a 150° angle in more than one way? Explain.

Staying Fit

Solve the story problems below. Be sure
to show your work and equations.

NOTE Students practice solving
multiplication and division problems
in a story problem context.

SMH 45

**Marisol's family decided to keep track
of how much they exercised during
April and May.**

1. **a.** Marisol's mother ran on 22 days in April. On each
   of those days, she ran 4 miles. How many miles did
   she run in April?

   b. In May, she increased her daily distance to 5 miles,
   and ran 19 days that month. How many miles did
   she run in May?

2. At the end of April and May, Marisol calculated that
   she had walked 3 miles every day for those 61 days.
   How many miles did she walk in April and May?

3. Marisol's father biked 190 miles in 5 days. He biked
   the same distance each day. How many miles did he
   bike each day?

Size, Shape, and Symmetry   Homework

Sorting Triangles

Write the numbers of all of the triangles that belong in each category. You may use the corner of a sheet of paper as a "right angle tester."

NOTE Students practice identifying angles and classifying triangles by their angle sizes.

SMH 111–113

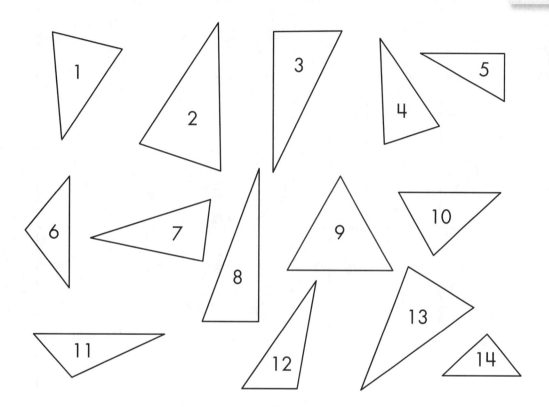

1. Which triangles have a right angle?

_____

2. Which triangles have 3 acute angles?

_____

3. Which triangles have 1 obtuse angle?

_____

Size, Shape, and Symmetry

Mystery Multiple Tower (page 1 of 2)

This is the top part of Anna's Multiple Tower. Answer these questions about her tower.

> **NOTE** Students practice solving multiplication and division problems in the context of a "tower" of multiples.
>
> **SMH** 36

168
154
140
126
112

1. What number did Anna count by? How do you know?

2. How many numbers are in Anna's tower so far? How do you know?

3. Write a multiplication equation that represents how many numbers are in Anna's Multiple Tower:

   _____ × _____ = _____

Mystery Multiple Tower (page 2 of 2)

4. What is the 10th multiple in Anna's tower?

5. Imagine that Anna adds more multiples to her tower.

   a. What would be the 20th multiple in her tower?
   How do you know?

   b. What would be the 25th multiple in her tower?
   How do you know?

Size, Shape, and Symmetry   Homework

Measuring Angles

Use the corner of a sheet of paper as a 90-degree angle to help you measure each of the angles below. You may also fold the corner of another sheet of paper in half to make a 45-degree angle with which to measure. Match each angle to one of the measures in the box. One measure is used twice.

> **NOTE** Students practice identifying angles of particular sizes.
>
> **SMH** 111, 112, 113

30°   45°   60°   90°   120°   135°   150°

1.

Angle Measure:

_____

2.

Angle Measure:

_____

3.

Angle Measure: _____

4.

Angle Measure: _____

5.

Angle Measure: _____

6.

Angle Measure: _____

7.

Angle Measure:

_____

8.

Angle Measure: _____

© Pearson Education 4

Directions for Making a Design

Work in pairs to make a symmetrical design.

1. Make a horizontal line of symmetry across the center of M23, Triangle Paper. One side will be Player 1's side; the other will be Player 2's side. Work only on your own side of the line.

2. Player 1 places a shape on the triangle paper, touching the line of symmetry on one side.

3. Player 2 puts the same kind of shape in the mirror-image position on the other side of the line.

4. Player 2 places a new shape on the paper. The shape must touch either the line of symmetry or at least one corner or side of a shape already placed.

5. Player 1 puts a shape in the mirror-image position of Player 2's shape.

6. Continue, until 12 shapes have been placed in all.

7. Set the first design to the side and start a new design on a separate sheet of Triangle Paper, following steps 1–6.

8. After you finish the second design, each player colors one of the designs. Use colors that match the Power Polygon piece.

Measuring Area with Triangles

Using the triangle piece, determine the area of each of the
designs that you made. How many triangles does it take to
cover the design?

1. Look at your first design. What is its area? _____

Explain how you determined its area.

2. Look at your second design. What is its area? _____

Explain how you determined its area.

Related Problems About Multiplying Groups of 10

NOTE Students practice solving multiplication problems about multiplying by multiples of 10.

SMH 37–38

Solve each pair of multiplication problems below.

1.

$9 \times 6 =$ _____

$9 \times 60 =$ _____

2.

$11 \times 5 =$ _____

$110 \times 5 =$ _____

3.

$15 \times 6 =$ _____

$15 \times 60 =$ _____

4.

$14 \times 4 =$ _____

$14 \times 40 =$ _____

5.

$7 \times 9 =$ _____

$7 \times 90 =$ _____

6.

$12 \times 6 =$ _____

$12 \times 60 =$ _____

7.

$5 \times 16 =$ _____

$50 \times 16 =$ _____

8.

$80 \times 5 =$ _____

$800 \times 5 =$ _____

Is It Symmetrical?

Look at each of the block letters below. Some of them have mirror symmetry and some of them do not. For each letter that has mirror symmetry, draw at least one line of symmetry. Can you find more than one line? If a letter does not have a line of symmetry, write "no" next to it.

NOTE Students practice looking for lines of symmetry.

SMH 117

1. **T**	2. **E**	3. **N**
4. **X**	5. **D**	6. **H**
7. **F**	8. **J**	9. **L**

What's the Area? (page 1 of 2)

Answer these questions.
Build this design with Power Polygons:

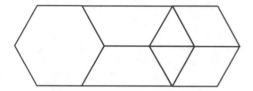

1. What is its area if you use triangles to cover it?

   Area: _____ triangles

2. What is its area if you use trapezoids to cover it?

   Area: _____ trapezoids

Build this design with Power Polygons:

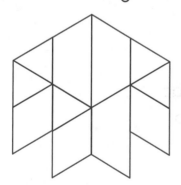

3. What is its area if you use triangles to cover it?

   Area: _____ triangles

4. What is its area if you use trapezoids to cover it?

   Area: _____ trapezoids

What's the Area? (page 2 of 2)

Answer these questions.

Build this design with Power Polygons:

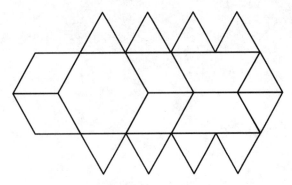

5. What is its area if you use triangles to cover it?

    Area: _____ triangles

6. What is its area if you use trapezoids to cover it?

    Area: _____ trapezoids

7. Compare the number of triangles it takes to cover each shape to the number of trapezoids it takes. What do you notice?

8. If you use hexagons instead of triangles to cover each shape, will it take more hexagons or fewer hexagons? Why do you think so?

Mirror Symmetry

For each figure that has mirror symmetry, draw the line(s) of symmetry.

NOTE Students identify and draw designs that have at least one line of symmetry.

SMH 117

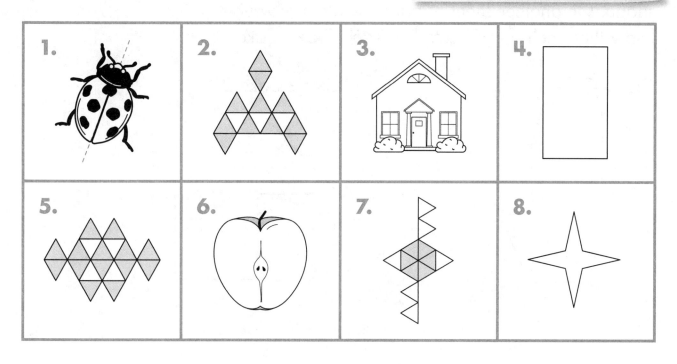

1.

2.

3.

4.

5.

6.

7.

8.

9. On triangle paper, draw a design that has mirror symmetry. You may color it if you like. How many lines of symmetry does your design have?

Ongoing Review

10. In which shape is the dotted line a line of symmetry?

A. 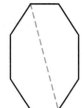   B.    C. 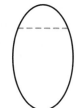   D.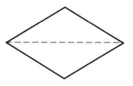

Crazy Cakes (page 1 of 2)

Divide each of the Crazy Cakes below into two equal halves. The two halves do not need to have the same shape. On another sheet of paper, explain how you know that each person gets $\frac{1}{2}$ of each Crazy Cake.

Crazy Cake 1

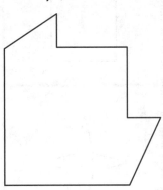

Crazy Cake 2

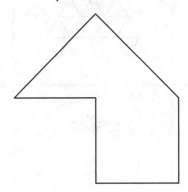

Crazy Cake 3

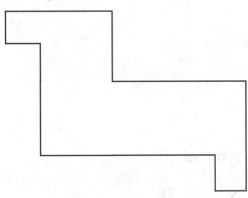

Crazy Cakes (page 2 of 2)

Divide each of the Crazy Cakes below into two equal halves. The two halves do not need to have the same shape. On another sheet of paper, explain how you know that each person gets $\frac{1}{2}$ of each Crazy Cake.

Crazy Cake 4

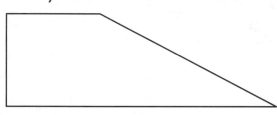

Crazy Cake 5

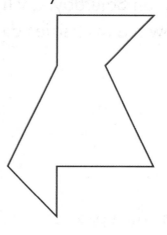

Crazy Cake 6

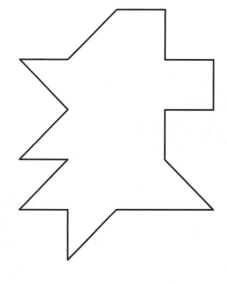

More Multiplication and Division Stories

> **NOTE** Students practice solving multiplication and division problems in a story problem context.
>
> SMH 45

Solve each problem and show your work.
Write an equation for each problem.

1. Ms. Thompson sold 6 cartons of cherries at the Farmers' Market on Saturday. Each carton holds 25 cherries. How many cherries did she sell?

2. On Sunday, Ms. Thompson sold 300 cherries. How many cartons of cherries did she sell on Sunday?

3. Ms. Thompson sells the cherries for $4 per pound. How many pounds of cherries could you buy for $50?

More Crazy Cakes

Divide each of the Crazy Cakes below into two equal halves. The two halves do not need to have the same shape. On another sheet of paper, for each cake, explain how you know that each person gets $\frac{1}{2}$ of each Crazy Cake.

NOTE Students divide a "crazy cake" so that each person sharing the cake would get half of the cake.

Crazy Cake 1

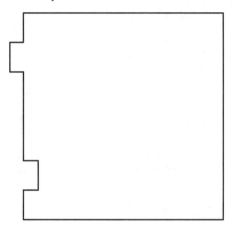

Crazy Cake 2

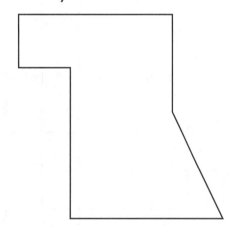

Crazy Cake 3

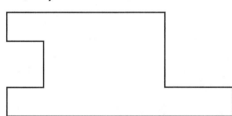

Size, Shape, and Symmetry

Measuring Area on
the Geoboard (page 1 of 2)

Find the area of each shape and explain how you found it.
It may be helpful to build the shape on your Geoboard.

1. Area: _____   Explain.

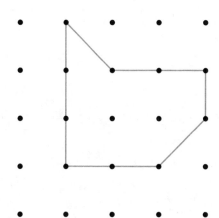

2. Area: _____   Explain.

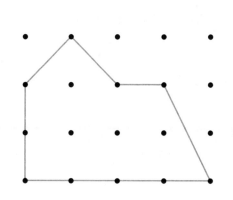

Size, Shape, and Symmetry

Measuring Area on the Geoboard (page 2 of 2)

Find the area of each shape and explain how you found it.
It may be helpful to build the shape on your Geoboard.

3. Area: _____   Explain.

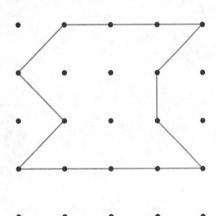

4. Area: _____   Explain.

Related Problems About Doubling and Halving

NOTE Students practice solving multiplication problems. Ask your child to explain any patterns he or she notices in each set of problems.

Solve each set of multiplication problems below.

1.

$8 \times 6 =$ _____

$16 \times 3 =$ _____

$4 \times 12 =$ _____

2.

$18 \times 8 =$ _____

$18 \times 4 =$ _____

$9 \times 8 =$ _____

3.

$9 \times 6 =$ _____

$18 \times 3 =$ _____

$18 \times 6 =$ _____

4.

$16 \times 3 =$ _____

$16 \times 6 =$ _____

$8 \times 12 =$ _____

5.

$15 \times 8 =$ _____

$30 \times 4 =$ _____

$60 \times 4 =$ _____

6.

$3 \times 21 =$ _____

$3 \times 42 =$ _____

$6 \times 42 =$ _____

Name _____ Date _____

That's Not Fair!

Draw an "X" on any shape that is not fairly divided into two equal halves.

> **NOTE** Students decide whether the two parts of irregular shapes have equal areas.

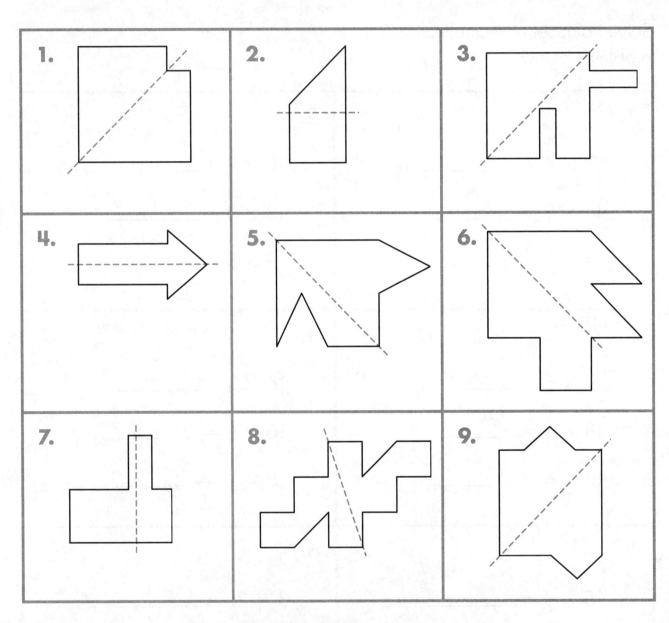

1.

2.

3.

4.

5.

6.

7.

8.

9.

10. Choose one of the shapes above that does not have equal halves and explain how you know.

Area of Rectangles (page 1 of 2)

The part of Mr. Frank's classroom that is tiled is covered with rugs. In the drawings below, each tile is one square foot. Find the area of each section of tiled floor. Explain how you got your answer.

1. Area: _____   Explain.

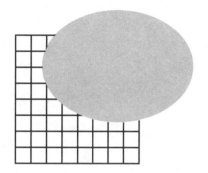

2. Area: _____   Explain.

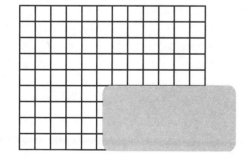

Area of Rectangles (page 2 of 2)

The part of Mr. Frank's classroom that is tiled is covered with rugs. In the drawings below, each tile is one square foot. Find the area of each section of tiled floor. Explain how you got your answer.

3. Area: _____   Explain.

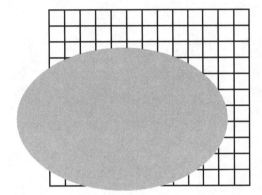

4. Area: _____   Explain.

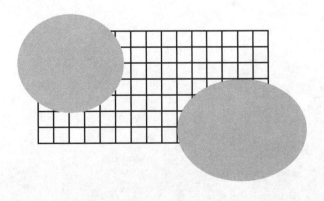

Big Square, Little Square

Find the number of unit squares in each part of the larger square.

NOTE Students find the area of polygons in square units.

SMH 114–115

 ⟵ 1 unit square (or 1 square unit)

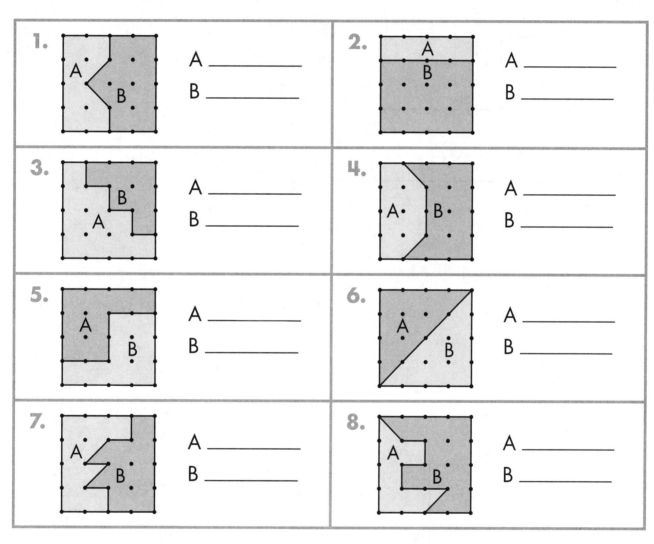

1. A _____
   B _____

2. A _____
   B _____

3. A _____
   B _____

4. A _____
   B _____

5. A _____
   B _____

6. A _____
   B _____

7. A _____
   B _____

8. A _____
   B _____

Ongoing Review

9. In which pair do the figures have equal areas?

A.   **B.**   **C.** 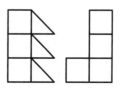 **D.**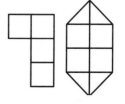

Area of Polygons (page 1 of 3)

Determine the area of the polygons shown.
Explain or show how you found the area.

1.

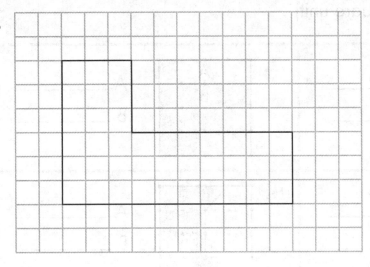

2.

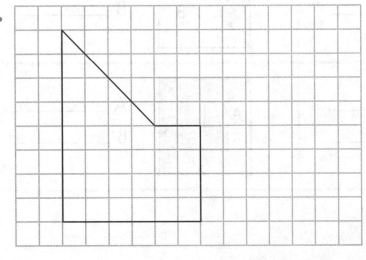

Size, Shape, and Symmetry

Area of Polygons (page 2 of 3)

Determine the area of the polygons shown.
Explain or show how you found the area.

3.

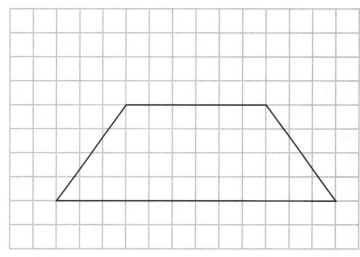

4.

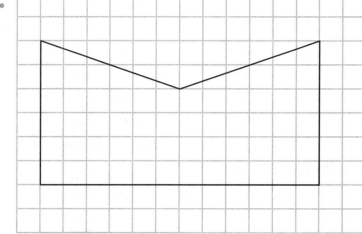

Area of Polygons (page 3 of 3)

Determine the area of the polygon shown.
Explain or show how you found the area.

5.

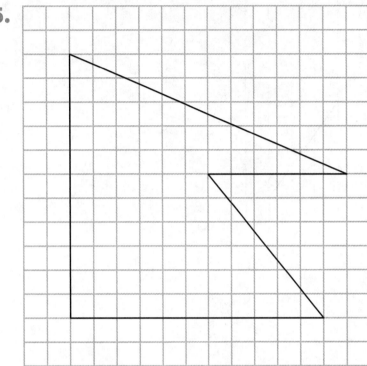

Area of 4

Color more spaces to make each shape have an area of 4 square units. Remember: Each shape must have touching gridlines.

NOTE Students create shapes that have an area of exactly 4 square units.

 SMH 115

1.
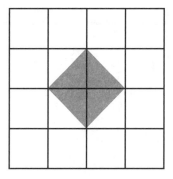

2.
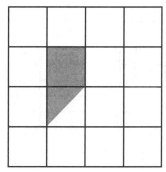

3.
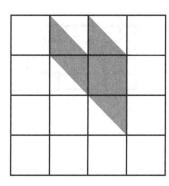

4.
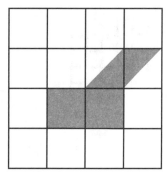

Ongoing Review

5. Which figure has an area of 6 square units if 1 square unit = ☐?

A.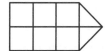

B.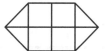

C.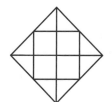

D.

Finding the Area of Rectangles

NOTE Students use area measurement to determine which is the larger of two rectangles in a pair.

 114

In each pair of rectangles, circle the rectangle that you think has the greater area. Then check by finding the area of each rectangle.

1.

2.

3.

4.

5.

6.

Pet Parade

Your neighborhood is getting ready for its annual Pet Parade. You are in charge of deciding the parade route. Design three different routes for the neighborhood to vote on at the parade meeting. The parade must begin and end at the park, and the route must be 20 blocks long.

NOTE Students solve real-world problems involving the math content of this unit.

The Neighborhood

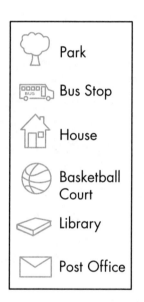

Park
Bus Stop
House
Basketball Court
Library
Post Office

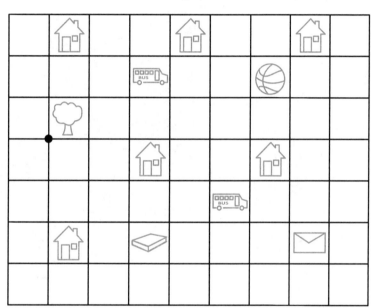

1 block

1 block

1. **Red Route**   The length of the red route is _____ blocks.

2. **Blue Route**   The length of the blue route is _____ blocks.

3. **Green Route**   The length of the green route is _____ blocks.

4. How many blocks would the parade need to go to see **all** of the places on the map?

5. What would the length of that route be?

Polished Spiral Karin Kuhlmann

"Although the creation of fractals is bounded to strict mathematical rules, the results are always very inspiring." – **Karin Kuhlmann**

Investigations
IN NUMBER, DATA, AND SPACE®

Landmarks and Large Numbers

What's the Number?

Write the number that matches each number written in words.

NOTE Students practice place value by writing numbers that match the words and by placing the numbers in order.

SMH 6

Example: two hundred ninety-eight ___298___

1. five hundred seven _____

2. three hundred thirteen _____

3. one hundred sixty-five _____

4. one hundred twelve _____

5. three hundred thirty-one _____

6. Place the five numbers above in order from least to greatest.

_____ _____ _____ _____ _____

Ongoing Review

7. Which is 10 **less than** 106?

   A. 6   **B.** 96   **C.** 100   **D.** 116

Find the Numbers

In your 1,000 book, find the correct square for each of the following numbers, and write the number in your book. For each number you write, tell which 100 chart it belongs in. (Remember that each chart is named by the last number, so the chart that ends in 400 is called the "400 chart.")

1. 45 is on the _____ chart

2. 192 is on the _____ chart

3. 850 is on the _____ chart

4. 375 is on the _____ chart

5. 799 is on the _____ chart

6. 467 is on the _____ chart

7. 903 is on the _____ chart

8. 513 is on the _____ chart

9. 222 is on the _____ chart

10. 631 is on the _____ chart

11. Choose one of the numbers above, and explain how you used your 1,000 book to find where that number belongs.

Factors and Products

Fill in the chart below with the missing factors or products. Can you solve some of these mentally?

NOTE Students practice multiplying and dividing.

SMH 45

Factor	×	Factor	=	Product
4	×	36	=	
2	×	72	=	
8	×		=	240
5	×		=	175
6	×	19	=	
8	×		=	96
7	×	60	=	
10	×		=	230
9	×	31	=	

Practicing Place Value

NOTE Every student has been making a 1,000 book to help read, write, and sequence numbers up to 1,000. This book can be used to complete this homework.

 SMH 6

Complete these equations. (You may use your 1,000 book to help you.)

1. 559 + 1 = _____

559 − 1 = _____

559 + 10 = _____

559 − 10 = _____

2. 101 + 1 = _____

101 − 1 = _____

101 + 10 = _____

101 − 10 = _____

3. 776 + 1 = _____

776 − 1 = _____

776 + 30 = _____

776 − 30 = _____

4. 899 + 1   = _____

899 − 1   = _____

899 + 100 = _____

899 − 100 = _____

5. If you counted by 100s, how many would it take to get to 500? How do you know?

6. If you counted by 10s, how many would it take to get to 500? How do you know?

7. If you counted by 10s, how many would it take to get to 330? How do you know?

Changing Places Recording Sheet

Record your starting number, the Change Cards you used, and an equation that shows the new number you made.

Remember that your new number is always your next starting number!

Starting Number	Change Cards	Equation
Example: 243	+10, −20, +100	243 + 10 − 20 + 100 = 333
1.		
2.		
3.		
4.		
5.		
6.		
7.		
8.		
9.		
10.		

Matching Runners' Numbers

Draw a line from each runner's number
to the words.

NOTE Students match
numbers with words and
place numbers in order.

SMH 6

1. 336   one hundred forty-eight

2. 901   three hundred thirty-six

3. 520   nine hundred seven

4. 148   five hundred twenty

5. 907   nine hundred one

6. Place the numbers above in order from the greatest
   to the least.

   _____ _____ _____ _____ _____

Ongoing Review

7. Which is 30 **more than** 387?

   A. 417   **B.** 407   **C.** 400   **D.** 357

Adding and Subtracting 10s and 100s

Solve the following problems and show your solutions.

NOTE Students have been working on an activity, "Changing Places," in which they add and subtract multiples of 10 and 100 to and from 3-digit numbers. This skill helps students become more efficient with computation.

1. $255 + 40 + 20 + 40 =$ _____

2. $909 - 400 - 80 - 100 =$ _____

3. $344 + 300 - 50 =$ _____

4. $789 - 200 + 200 + 20 =$ _____

How Many Miles to 1,000? (page 1 of 2)

Imagine that you are taking a road trip that will be exactly 1,000 miles. For each problem below, find how many more miles you need to go to get to 1,000 miles. Explain how you solved the problem.

1. You have traveled 325 miles. How many more miles to 1,000? This is how I solved the problem:

2. You have traveled 485 miles. How many more miles to 1,000? This is how I solved the problem:

3. You have traveled 540 miles. How many more miles to 1,000? This is how I solved the problem:

4. You have traveled 673 miles. How many more miles to 1,000? This is how I solved the problem:

5. You have traveled 812 miles. How many more miles to 1,000? This is how I solved the problem:

How Many Miles to 1,000? (page 2 of 2)

For each problem, draw three Digit Cards to make a number in the hundreds. Find how many more miles you need to go to get to 1,000 miles. Explain how you solved the problem.

6. You have traveled _____ miles. How many more miles to 1,000?
This is how I solved the problem:

7. You have traveled _____ miles. How many more miles to 1,000?
This is how I solved the problem:

8. You have traveled _____ miles. How many more miles to 1,000?
This is how I solved the problem:

9. You have traveled _____ miles. How many more miles to 1,000?
This is how I solved the problem:

10. You have traveled _____ miles. How many more miles to 1,000?
This is how I solved the problem:

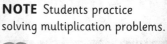

Multiplication Problems

Solve each of the problems below.
Show your thinking.

NOTE Students practice solving multiplication problems.

 SMH 40, 41, 42

1. 27 × 5 = _____

2. 43 × 4 = _____

3. 6 × 29 = _____

4. 34 × 5 = _____

5. 30 × 26 = _____

6. 12 × 51 = _____

Ongoing Review

7. 14 × 32 = _____

 A. 160 **B.** 328 **C.** 334 **D.** 448

Landmarks and Large Numbers

The Jones Family's Trip

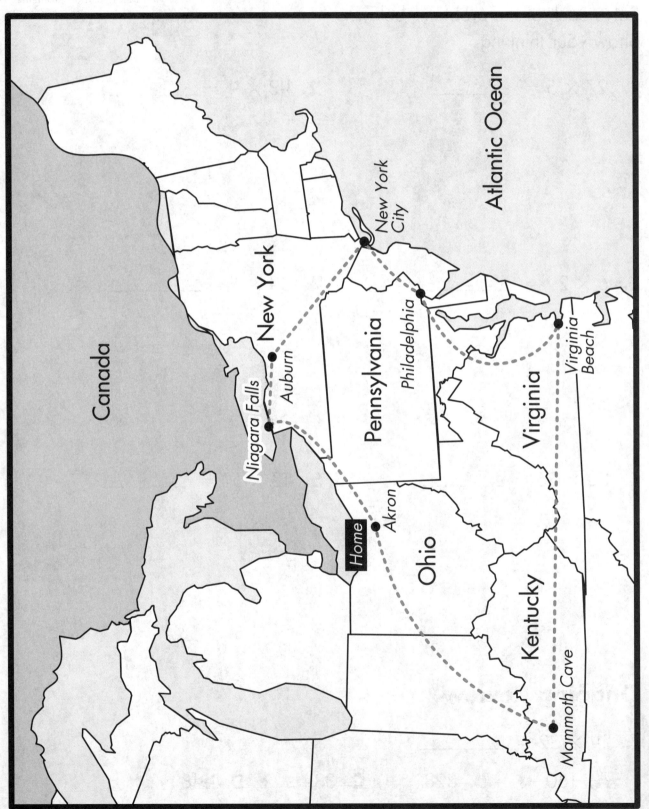

Atlantic Ocean

Canada

New York

New York City

Pennsylvania

Philadelphia

Auburn

Niagara Falls

Virginia

Virginia Beach

Home

Akron

Ohio

Kentucky

Mammoth Cave

How Many Miles?

Solve these problems about the Jones family's car trip.
Show your solutions so that someone else can understand
how you solved the problem.

1. In the first week of their trip, the Jones family drove
   427 miles from their home in Ohio to Mammoth Cave
   in Kentucky. After their visit there, they drove 733 miles
   to Virginia Beach. How many miles did they drive
   altogether?

2. In the second week, the Jones family drove 270 miles
   from Virginia Beach to Philadelphia, Pennsylvania, to
   see the Liberty Bell. From Philadelphia, they drove to
   New York City, which is 96 miles away. How many
   miles did they drive altogether from Virginia Beach to
   New York City?

3. In the third week, the Jones family went to two more
   places in New York state. They drove 259 miles to see
   the Harriet Tubman House in Auburn, New York, and
   then 138 more miles to see Niagara Falls. Then it was
   time to go home, which was 235 miles away from
   Niagara Falls. How many miles did the Jones family
   drive in the third week of their trip?

Count Your Change Carefully

NOTE Students practice subtraction in the context of money and receiving change.

SMH 13–15

Complete this chart.

Item	Cost of Item	Amount Given to Clerk	Amount of Change
1. Ruler	$0.47	$1.00	
2. Sandwich	$3.18	$5.00	
3. Seeds	$1.55		$0.45
4. Socks	$2.74		$2.26
5. Shampoo		$1.00	$0.11
6. Apple		$5.00	$4.10
7. Stickers	$1.16	$10.00	
8. Magazine		$10.00	$6.35

Ongoing Review

9. 255 + _____ = 1,000

A. 755   **B.** 750   **C.** 745   **D.** 705

© Pearson Education 4

Addition Problems

Solve the following addition problems and show your solutions. (Try to use a new strategy that you learned in class today.)

NOTE Students practice strategies for solving addition problems.

SMH 8–9

1. At the Harriet Tubman House in Auburn, the Jones family spent $9.45 for all their admission tickets and $6.99 for a book about Tubman's life. How much money did they spend at the Harriet Tubman House?

2. 488 + 522 = _____

3. 534
      + 323
      ――――

More Addition Problems

Solve the following addition problems and show your solutions. (Try to use a strategy that you have not tried before.)

1. The Jones family stopped at a pizza place for supper. They ordered a large pizza that cost $12.95. They also shared a salad that cost $7.49. How much did supper cost that night?

2. While they were driving, Mrs. Jones gave Donte this problem to solve: $458 + 548$. His answer was 1,006. Did he get the right answer? How would you solve it?

3. $457 + 776 = $ _____

4. 1,397
   $+ \ 663$

Solving Addition Problems

Solve each addition problem.
Show your work clearly.

NOTE Students practice solving addition problems.

SMH 8–9

1. $639 + 541 = $ _____

2. $775 + 541 = $ _____

3.   186
      +805
      ‾‾‾‾

Ongoing Review

4. Which number does **not** have a 7 in the ones place?

A. 7   **B.** 17   **C.** 470   **D.** 977

More Addition Problems

Solve the following addition problems and show your solutions.

NOTE Students continue to solve addition problems.

SMH 8–9

1. Tara saved $143 from babysitting and opened a bank account. During the year, she put $829 more in the account. How much money did she have in the bank at the end of the year?

2. Marcos went to the store to buy materials for his science fair project. The poster board cost $7.99 and the packet of construction paper cost $2.49. How much money did he spend?

3. 536 + 887 = _____

Addition Starter Problems (page 1 of 2)

In Problems 1–6, solve all three starter problems. Then choose one of the starter problems and use it to solve the final problem. Put a star next to the starter problem that you used and show how you finished the problem.

1. $300 + 500 =$ _____ $315 + 500 =$ _____ $315 + 5 =$ _____

   Choose one of the starter problems above and use it to solve this problem:

   $315 + 566 =$

2. $288 + 400 =$ _____ $200 + 400 =$ _____ $300 + 450 =$ _____

   Choose one of the starter problems above and use it to solve this problem:

   $288 + 456 =$

3. $597 + 300 =$ _____ $600 + 375 =$ _____ $600 + 372 =$ _____

   Choose one of the starter problems above and use it to solve this problem:

   $597 + 375 =$

Addition Starter Problems (page 2 of 2)

4. $\$9.94 + \$5.00 = $ ___ $\$9.00 + \$5.00 = $ ___ $\$0.94 + \$0.06 = $ ___

Choose one of the starter problems above and use it to solve
this problem:

$\$9.94 + \$5.16 = $

5. $500 + 300 + 200 = $ ___ $532 + 300 + 200 = $ ___

$530 + 370 = $ ___

Choose one of the starter problems above and use it to solve
this problem:

$$
\begin{array}{r}
1,532 \\
2,371 \\
+\ 212 \\
\hline
\end{array}
$$

6. $785 + 400 = $ ___ $800 + 428 = $ ___ $785 + 15 = $ ___

Choose one of the starter problems above and use it to solve
this problem:

$785 + 428 = $

Related Problems About Multiplying Groups of 10

NOTE Students practice solving multiplication problems and explain any patterns about multiplying groups of 10 that they notice in each pair of problems.

SMH 37–38

Solve each pair of multiplication problems below.

1. 8×6 = _____

8×60 = _____

2. 7×7 = _____

7×70 = _____

3. 9×7 = _____

90×7 = _____

4. 12×8 = _____

120×8 = _____

5. 15×5 = _____

15×50 = _____

6. 6×13 = _____

60×13 = _____

7. 11×4 = _____

11×40 = _____

8. 60×5 = _____

600×5 = _____

Ongoing Review

9. Which is 400 less than 866?

   A. 862   **B.** 826   **C.** 466   **D.** 422

How Do You Solve an Addition Problem?

NOTE Students practice solving addition problems. Share with your child how you would solve the problem.

SMH **8–10**

To the student:

1. Solve this problem and show your solution:

$$299 + 156 = \underline{\hspace{3cm}}$$

To the adult:

2. How would you solve this problem? Please record your solution. (If you solved the problem mentally, explain what you did.)

$$\begin{array}{r} 299 \\ +156 \\ \hline \end{array}$$

3. Is this the way you were taught to solve addition problems when you were in school? If not, solve it the way you were taught.

$$\begin{array}{r} 299 \\ +156 \\ \hline \end{array}$$

Two Different Solutions

1. Solve this problem. Show your solution,
   using clear and concise notation.

   $145 + 226 = $ _____

   Now look carefully at these two different solutions for
   the same problem. Answer the questions below.

   Solution 1

   $$\begin{array}{r} 145 \\ +226 \\ \hline 300 \\ 60 \\ +\ 11 \\ \hline 371 \end{array}$$

   Solution 2

   $$\begin{array}{r} \overset{1}{1}45 \\ +226 \\ \hline 371 \end{array}$$

2. How would you explain to someone else how
   Solution 1 works? (Where does the 60 come
   from? Where does the 11 come from?)

3. How would you explain to someone else how
   Solution 2 works? (Where does the 1 above
   the 4 in 145 come from?)

Solving an Addition Problem in Two Ways

NOTE Students practice strategies for addition by solving a problem in two ways.

SMH 8–9

1. Solve this problem in two different ways. Be sure to show how you got your answer.

   $431 + 799 =$ _____

   Here is the first way I solved it:

   Here is the second way I solved it:

Ongoing Review

2. Which of the following is true?

   A. $11 + 880 > 1,000$ **C.** $733 + 218 > 1,000$

   B. $642 + 419 > 1,000$ **D.** $82 + 904 > 1,000$

Close to 1,000 Recording Sheet

Game 1   **Score**

Round 1: _____ _____ _____ + _____ _____ _____ = _____   _____

Round 2: _____ _____ _____ + _____ _____ _____ = _____   _____

Round 3: _____ _____ _____ + _____ _____ _____ = _____   _____

Round 4: _____ _____ _____ + _____ _____ _____ = _____   _____

Round 5: _____ _____ _____ + _____ _____ _____ = _____   _____

Final Score _____

Game 2   **Score**

Round 1: _____ _____ _____ + _____ _____ _____ = _____   _____

Round 2: _____ _____ _____ + _____ _____ _____ = _____   _____

Round 3: _____ _____ _____ + _____ _____ _____ = _____   _____

Round 4: _____ _____ _____ + _____ _____ _____ = _____   _____

Round 5: _____ _____ _____ + _____ _____ _____ = _____   _____

Final Score _____

Apple Orchard

Solve the story problems below. Show your work and your equations.

NOTE Students practice solving multiplication and division problems in story problem contexts.

SMH 45

1. At an apple orchard, small bags contain 7 apples. Alexa and her family bought 91 apples for a party. How many small bags did they buy?

2. Large bags hold 14 apples. When a fourth-grade class went apple picking, they filled 9 large bags. How many apples did they pick?

3. Savanna and her three brothers picked 55 apples. They shared the apples equally among the four of them. How many apples did each child get? Were there any apples left over?

Adding to 1,000

Fill in the missing number in each equation.
Show how you found the missing number.

NOTE Students create addition
problems that add to 1,000.

SMH 8–9

1. $1,000 = 635 + \underline{\hspace{2cm}}$

2. $\quad\quad 289$
$\quad + \underline{\hspace{2cm}}$
$\quad\quad 1,000$

3. $\underline{\hspace{2cm}} + 543 = 1,000$

Related Problems About Doubling and Halving

NOTE Students practice solving multiplication problems. Ask your child to explain any patterns he or she notices in each set of problems.

SMH 43

Solve each set of multiplication problems below.

1. 4 × 7 = _____

    8 × 7 = _____

    8 × 14 = _____

2. 6 × 9 = _____

    12 × 9 = _____

    6 × 18 = _____

3. 3 × 11 = _____

    6 × 11 = _____

    6 × 22 = _____

4. 5 × 8 = _____

    10 × 8 = _____

    20 × 8 = _____

5. 3 × 15 = _____

    3 × 30 = _____

    6 × 15 = _____

6. 32 × 4 = _____

    16 × 8 = _____

    8 × 8 = _____

Choose Wisely

Add the number in the first box to each of the other two numbers. Draw the path that gets you closest to 1,000.

NOTE Students practice adding numbers whose total is near 1,000.

SMH 8–9

Example:

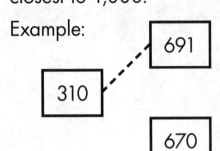

I chose 691 because 310 + 691 = 1,001, but 310 + 670 = 980.

1.

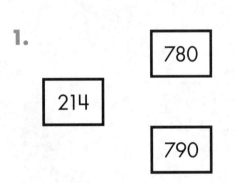

	780
214	
	790

2.

	515
480	
	522

3.

	545
555	
	555

4.

	199
807	
	203

Ongoing Review

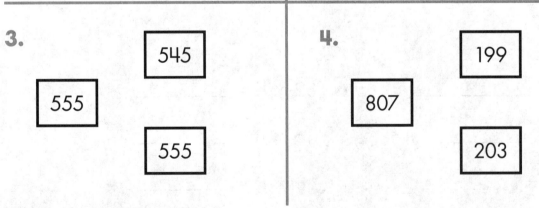

5. Which number could be read as "thirteen hundred"?

   A. 130   **B.** 1,003   **C.** 1,013   **D.** 1,300

Problems About *Close to 1,000*

Solve these problems and show your work.

1. What is the difference between 425 and 1,000?

2. How much more is 1,662 than 1,000?

3. Do 768 and 222 added together make 1,000? If not, what is the difference between the sum and 1,000?

How Many 10s Are in 10,000?

From your work on the 10,000 chart, you know that:

There are ten 1,000s in 10,000.
There are one hundred 100s in 10,000.

How would you explain to a third-grade student
how many 10s there are in 10,000?

Write your explanation on a separate sheet of paper. You
may write it as a letter to a third-grade student if you wish.
You may also include any pictures or equations that you
think will help make your explanation clearer.

Pick a Number

The first and last numbers of some 100 charts are shown. Write another number that belongs on each chart.

NOTE Students practice finding a number on 100 charts.

SMH **6**

1.

1,201

_____

1,300

2.

2,401

_____

2,500

3.

3,501

_____

3,600

4.

5,901

_____

6,000

5.

7,701

_____

7,800

6.

9,001

_____

9,100

Ongoing Review

7. Which number is between 4,009 and 4,156?

A. 4,005   **B.** 4,056   **C.** 4,160   **D.** 4,500

Changing Places on the 10,000 Chart

For these problems, choose **one** Change Card and make a new number. Write an equation that shows your new number.

Starting Number	Change Card	Equation
Example: 398	+100	398 + 100 = 498
1. 4,159		
2. 510		
3. 924		
4. 2,790		
5. Choose a number. _____		

For these problems, choose **two** Change Cards and make a new number. Write an equation that shows your new number.

Starting Number	Change Cards	Equation
Example: 496	+10, −100	496 + 10 − 100 = 406
6. 227		
7. 778		
8. 1,250		
9. 6,421		
10. Choose a number. _____		

Division Stories

Solve each problem below. Show your work.
Write a division equation for each problem.

NOTE Students practice solving division problems in story problem contexts.

SMH 50–52

1. A theater ticket costs $8. How many tickets can you buy for $128?

2. One row in the theater has 12 seats. If 132 students go to see a play at the theater, how many rows of seats can they fill up?

3. If 132 students ride to the theater in vans, and 6 students can ride in each van, how many vans will they need?

Ongoing Review

4. Which expression is **less than** 500?

   A. 490 + 80 − 30 − 10 − 10   **C.** 595 − 200 + 300

   B. 868 − 400 + 20   **D.** 420 + 300 − 100 − 90

All About the Number (page 1 of 2)

Answer the following questions about the number 4,736.

NOTE Students are making a 10,000 chart to help them understand how our number system is constructed and to see important relationships within the number system. This homework focuses on these relationships, such as place value and "landmark numbers" (multiples of 10 and 100).

SMH 6

1. Is 4,736 closer to 4,000 or 5,000? How do you know?

2. Choose a landmark number that is close to 4,736.

3. Does 4,736 come before or after that landmark number?

4. What is 300 more than 4,736?

All About the Number (page 2 of 2)

5. What is 50 less than 4,736?

6. If I put 4,736 marbles into groups of 100, how many groups would I have? Show how you figured it out.

7. If I put 4,736 marbles into groups of 10, how many groups would I have? Show how you figured it out.

Landmarks and Large Numbers

Cities Around the U.S.

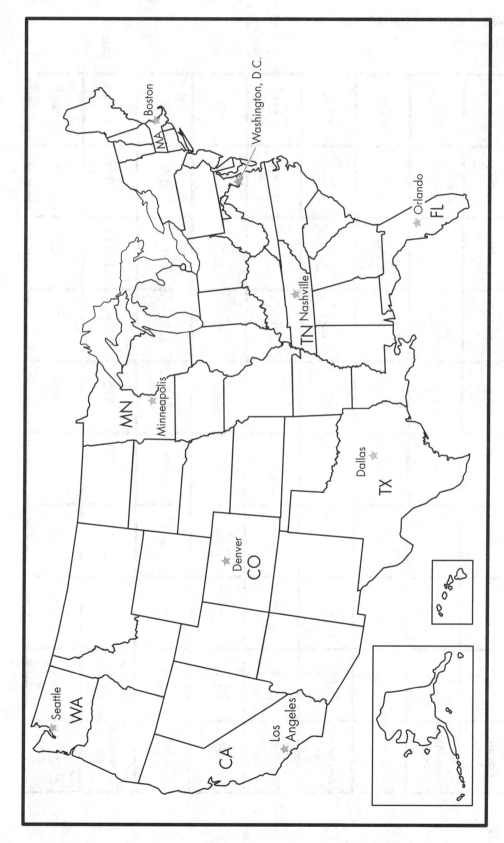

Landmarks and Large Numbers

City to City: How Many Miles?

This table shows driving distances between various U.S. cities.

	Boston, MA	Washington, D.C.	Orlando, FL	Nashville, TN	Minneapolis, MN	Dallas, TX	Denver, CO	Los Angeles, CA	Seattle, WA
Seattle, WA	3,046	2,764	3,135	2,450	1,658	2,202	1,332	1,138	0
Los Angeles, CA	2,984	2,655	2,513	2,006	1,928	1,434	1,018	0	1,138
Denver, CO	1,970	1,671	1,842	1,157	915	879	0	1,018	1,332
Dallas, TX	1,816	1,329	1,090	664	990	0	879	1,434	2,202
Minneapolis, MN	1,389	1,107	1,568	884	0	990	915	1,928	1,685
Nashville, TN	1,154	666	688	0	884	664	1,157	2,006	2,450
Orlando, FL	1,300	852	0	688	1,568	1,090	1,842	2,513	3,135
Washington, D.C.	446	0	852	666	1,107	1,329	1,671	2,655	2,764
Boston, MA	0	446	1,300	1,154	1,389	1,816	1,970	2,984	3,046

Landmarks and Large Numbers

Planning a Road Trip

From your map of the United States, choose at least 3 cities for your complete road trip. Use the table on page 46 to find the distance between the cities on your trip. Make an addition problem about how far you will travel on your trip, and solve the problem. Show your solution.

Trip 1

1. Where will you start your trip? _____

2. What city (or cities) will you visit? _____

3. Where will you finish your trip? _____

4. How many miles is your road trip altogether?
   Show how you figured it out.

Trip 2

5. Where will you start your trip? _____

6. What city (or cities) will you visit? _____

7. Where will you finish your trip? _____

8. How many miles is your road trip altogether?
   Show how you figured it out.

Changing Place Values

Solve each problem, showing your solutions clearly. Then write which place value(s) in the first number changed.

NOTE Students add and subtract 10s, 100s, and 1,000s to and from multi-digit numbers and determine which place values have changed.

SMH 6

1. $6{,}652 + 600 + 1{,}000 =$

   Which place value(s) changed? _____

2. $3{,}719 - 2{,}000 + 50 =$

   Which place value(s) changed? _____

3. $9{,}006 - 800 + 300 =$

   Which place value(s) changed? _____

Ongoing Review

4. How many 1,000s are in 8,008?

   A. 8   **B.** 80   **C.** 800   **D.** 8,000

Broken Calculator

Find five solutions to each of these problems.

1. I want to make 35 by using my calculator, but the 3 key and the 5 key are broken. How can I use my calculator to do this task?

2. I want to make 100 by using my calculator, but the 0 key and the $+$ key are broken. How can I use my calculator to do this task?

3. I want to make 48 by using my calculator, but the 4 key and the 8 key are broken. How can I use my calculator to do this task?

4. I want to make 99 by using my calculator, but the 9 key, the $+$ key, and the $-$ key are broken. How can I use my calculator to do this task?

5. I want to make 500 by using my calculator, but the 5 key, the $+$ key, and the $-$ key are broken. How can I use my calculator to do this task?

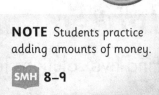

What's for Lunch?

Look at the menu below and imagine that you are ordering lunch for yourself and a friend. Choose at least 5 things. (Two could be drinks.) Write an addition problem about how much this lunch will cost and solve the problem. Show your solution.

NOTE Students practice adding amounts of money.

SMH 8-9

Joe's Cafe

Tacos	$5.38	**Drinks:**	
Hamburger	$4.59	Lemonade	$1.52
Chicken Soup	$2.06	Orange Juice	$1.79
Greek Salad	$4.79	Milk	$1.25
Tuna Sandwich	$3.43	Spring Water	$1.52
Peanut Butter and			
Jelly Sandwich	$3.65		
Egg Rolls	$2.26		
French Fries	$1.98		

1. What will you order for lunch?

2. How much will your lunch cost?

Subtraction Story Problems (page 1 of 2)

In Problems 1–6, draw a picture or number line or use your 1,000 book to show what is happening in the story. Then solve each problem and show your solutions.

1. Jamie's family visited their grandmother, who lives 634 miles from their house. On the first day, they drove 319 miles. How many miles did they have left to drive the second day?

2. Mr. Rivera and Ms. Santos each drove from Boston to other cities. Mr. Rivera drove 446 miles to Washington, D.C. Ms. Santos drove 1,300 miles to Orlando. How many more miles did Ms. Santos drive?

3. Ms. Jones took a trip from Washington, D.C., to Dallas, which is 1,329 miles away. She stopped in Nashville, which is 666 miles from Washington, D.C., and then drove to Dallas. How many miles did she drive from Nashville to Dallas?

Subtraction Story Problems (page 2 of 2)

4. Andreas had 475 basketball cards in his collection. He gave 89 cards to his younger brother for his birthday. How many cards does Andreas have left?

5. Natasha had $8.72. She spent $4.89 on a gift for her mother. How much money does Natasha have left?

6. Riverside School has 557 girls and 463 boys. How many more girls than boys are there at the school?

Subtraction Problems

Solve each subtraction problem.
Show your work clearly.

NOTE Students practice solving subtraction problems.

 SMH 13–15

1. 1,200 − 635 = _____

2. 884 − 591 = _____

3.   711
       −258
       ‾‾‾‾‾

Ongoing Review

4. Which of the following is true?

   A. 618 − 117 < 500

   C. 956 − 455 > 500

   B. 733 − 234 > 500

   D. 876 − 375 < 500

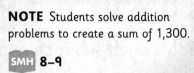

Close to 1,300

Read the story below and answer the questions.

NOTE Students solve addition problems to create a sum of 1,300.

SMH 8–9

> Robert and Leslie are playing a game they made up called *Close to 1,300*. The object of the game, as in *Close to 1,000*, is to make two numbers that total as close to 1,300 as possible.

1. Robert made this combination:

   937 + 365

   What is Robert's total? _____

2. Leslie made this combination:

   424 + 856

   What is Leslie's total? _____

3. Who is closer to 1,300? _____

4. What is each person's score? (Remember that the score is the difference between the total and 1,300.)

   Robert's score: _____   Leslie's score: _____

Date

Solving Subtraction Problems (page 1 of 2)

Solve each problem and show your solution.

1. $631 - 268 = $ _____

2. $\begin{array}{r} 704 \\ -551 \\ \hline \end{array}$

3. Jenna has 826 stamps in her collection. Ricardo has 637 stamps in his collection. How many more stamps does Jenna have?

Landmarks and Large Numbers

Solving Subtraction Problems (page 2 of 2)

4. The Diamond Egg Farm had 1,321 chickens. Last month they sold 663 of them to another farm. How many chickens do they have left?

5. In 1985, the population of West Littlebury was 1,877 people. In 2005, the population was 2,391 people. By how many people did the population of West Littlebury increase from 1985 to 2005?

6. $4,495 - 2,504 =$ _____

What's the Story?

Write a story to go with each problem. Then solve the problem and show your solution.

1. 947
   −182
   _____

2. 1,253 − 940 = _____

3. 714 − 399 = _____

What Should We Do with the Extras?

NOTE Students practice solving division problems and interpreting remainders in story problem contexts.

SMH 48, 49

Solve the problems below. Make sure that you keep track of all the steps you take. Write equations to show the steps of your solution.

1. Joey and his aunt picked 96 apples at the orchard. They plan to put them in bags of 8 apples each. How many bags of apples can they fill?

   Division equation: ___96___ ÷ ___8___ = _____   Answer: _____ bags

2. Five friends earned $72 from washing cars. They want to share the money equally among the five of them. How much money will each of the friends receive?

   Division equation: _____ ÷ _____ = _____   Answer: _____

3. Glue sticks come in packages of five. The art teacher at the Glendale School needs 72 glue sticks in her classroom. How many packages of glue sticks will she need to buy?

   Division equation: _____ ÷ _____ = _____   Answer: _____

Addition Practice

Solve the problems below and
show your solutions.

NOTE Students continue to
practice adding 3-digit numbers.

SMH 8–9

1. $\begin{array}{r} 272 \\ +354 \\ \hline \end{array}$

2. 768 + 843 = _____

3. Cesar took his mom out to lunch. They shared a pizza,
    which cost $9.78, and a salad, which cost $4.29. They
    drank water with their meal. Then Cesar's mom had
    coffee, which cost $1.10. How much did Cesar spend
    for lunch?

Events at the Community Center

Many events are held at the community center. Here are some events and the attendance at these events.

NOTE Students solve addition and subtraction problems in a story context.

SMH 8–9, 13–15

Event	Attendance
Science Fair	368
Basketball Tournament	741
Book Fair	555
Swim Meet	496
Rock Concert	1,152
Homecoming Dance	783

1. What was the total attendance of the science fair and the rock concert?

2. Which event had more people in attendance, the homecoming dance or the swim meet? How many more?

3. **a.** Which 3 events had the highest attendance?

   b. What was the total attendance at those 3 events?

Subtraction Starter Problems

In each set of problems below, solve all three starter
problems. Then choose one of the starter problems, and
use it to solve the final problem. Put a star next to the
starter problem that you used, and show how you
finished the problem.

1. $97 - 40 =$ _____ $97 - 30 =$ _____ $100 - 39 =$ _____

Choose one of the starter problems above and use it to
solve this problem:

$97 - 39 =$

2. $150 - 80 =$ _____ $150 - 75 =$ _____ $78 + 22 =$ _____

Choose one of the starter problems above and use it to
solve this problem:

$150 - 78 =$

3. $413 - 300 =$ _____ $413 - 200 =$ _____ $295 + 5 =$ _____

Choose one of the starter problems above and use it to
solve this problem:

$413 - 295 =$

Solving a Subtraction Problem in Two Ways

NOTE Students practice strategies for subtraction by solving a problem in two ways.

SMH 13–15

1. Solve this problem in two different ways. Be sure to show how you got your answer.

$487 - 209 =$ _____

Here is the first way I solved it:

Here is the second way I solved it:

Ongoing Review

2. $319 +$ _____ $= 1,000$

A. 596   **B.** 681   **C.** 785   **D.** 81

Subtraction Practice

Solve the problems below and show your solutions.

NOTE Students practice
solving subtraction problems.
SMH 13–15

1. 667 − 358 = _____

2.
$$\begin{array}{r} 515 \\ -472 \\ \hline \end{array}$$

3. Isabel has a stamp collection. She has 783 stamps so
far. Her goal is to collect 1,200 stamps. How many
more stamps does she need to reach her goal?

Landmarks and Large Numbers

Which Is Farther?
How Much Farther? (page 1 of 2)

For each pair of cities below, look at the information on page 46 and write the distance between them. Then, circle the distance that is farther, answer the question "How much farther?", and show your solution.

1. Which is farther: Orlando to Minneapolis?

   _____
   (Write the distance here.)

   or

   Orlando to Denver?

   _____
   (Write the distance here.)

   How much farther?

2. Which is farther: Dallas to Seattle?

   _____
   (Write the distance here.)

   or

   Dallas to Boston?

   _____
   (Write the distance here.)

   How much farther?

3. Which is farther: Los Angeles to Washington, D.C.?

   _____
   (Write the distance here.)

   or

   Los Angeles to Minneapolis?

   _____
   (Write the distance here.)

   How much farther?

© Pearson Education 4

Which Is Farther?
How Much Farther? (page 2 of 2)

Look at the chart on page 46. Choose two cities and write the distance between them.

4. Which is farther: _____ to _____? _____
   (city)   (city)   (Write the distance here.)

   or

   _____ to _____? _____
   (city)   (city)   (Write the distance here.)

   How much farther?

5. Which is farther: _____ to _____? _____
   (city)   (city)   (Write the distance here.)

   or

   _____ to _____? _____
   (city)   (city)   (Write the distance here.)

   How much farther?

6. Which is farther: _____ to _____? _____
   (city)   (city)   (Write the distance here.)

   or

   _____ to _____? _____
   (city)   (city)   (Write the distance here.)

   How much farther?

Money Problems (page 1 of 2)

Solve the problems below and show your solutions.

1. Ms. Chung went to the grocery store with $25.00 in her wallet. When she was finished shopping, she had $8.37. How much did the groceries cost?

2. Emily is saving to buy a desk and chair for her room. The desk costs $69.50. The chair costs $52.89. Emily has saved $39.40 so far. How much more does she need to save?

3. $262.51
   −$121.95
   _____

Money Problems (page 2 of 2)

4. Mr. Ortega took Ruben out for ice cream. Their ice cream cones cost $2.59 each. Mr. Ortega paid for both ice cream cones with a $10.00 bill. How much change did he receive?

5. Both John's and Eva's classes are collecting cans for recycling to raise money for a class trip. John's class has earned $46.30. Eva's class has earned $37.85. How much more money has John's class earned?

6. $30.52 + $18.78 + $43.22 = _____

More Subtraction Starter Problems

NOTE Students solve subtraction problems using different starts.
SMH 13–15

In each set of problems below, solve all three starter problems. Then choose one of the starter problems, and use it to solve the final problem. Put a star next to the starter problem that you used and show how you finished the solution.

1. $300 - 100 =$ _____ $363 - 100 =$ _____ $363 - 130 =$ _____

   Choose one of the starter problems above and use it to solve this problem:

   $363 - 129 =$

2. $805 - 600 =$ _____ $805 - 700 =$ _____ $694 + 6 =$ _____

   Choose one of the starter problems above and use it to solve this problem:

   $805 - 694 =$

Ongoing Review

3. Which expression is closest to 1,300?

   A. $685 + 735$ **C.** $653 + 612$

   B. $903 + 405$ **D.** $1,234 + 142$

Mystery Tower (page 1 of 2)

The picture shows the top part of Richard's multiple tower. Answer these questions about his tower.

NOTE Students practice solving multiplication and division problems.

SMH **36**

1. What number did Richard count by? How do you know?

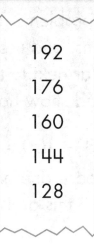

192

176

160

144

128

2. How many numbers are in Richard's tower so far? How do you know?

3. Write a multiplication equation that represents how many numbers are in Richard's multiple tower.

_____ × _____ = _____

Mystery Tower (page 2 of 2)

4. What is the 10th multiple in Richard's tower?

5. Imagine that Richard adds more multiples to his tower.

   a. What would be the 20th multiple in his tower?
   How do you know?

   b. What would be the 25th multiple in his tower?
   How do you know?

Ongoing Review

6. 8,350 − 400 + 60 = _____

   A. 8,110   **B.** 8,100   **C.** 8,010   **D.** 8,001

NOTE Students practice solving both addition and subtraction problems.

SMH 8–9, 13–15

Addition and Subtraction Practice

Solve the problems below and show your solutions.

1. The U.S. Olympic Soccer Team played in several cities around the United States. They played their first game in Los Angeles, and then flew to Denver, which is 1,018 miles away. After the Denver game, they flew to Dallas, which is 879 miles from Denver. How many miles has the team traveled?

2. A new player joined the team. She flew straight from Los Angeles to Dallas, which is 1,434 miles away. How many fewer miles did she travel than the team?

Shark Attack! (page 1 of 2)

Shown below are sharks found around the world
and their typical weights, in pounds.

NOTE Students practice
solving both addition and
subtraction problems.

 **8–9, 11–12, 13,
14, 15**

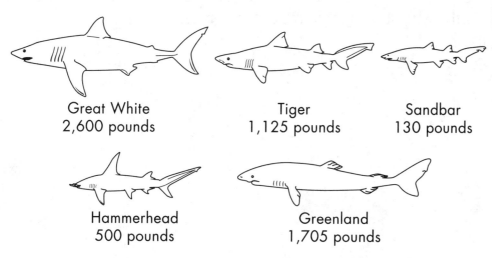

Great White
2,600 pounds

Tiger
1,125 pounds

Sandbar
130 pounds

Hammerhead
500 pounds

Greenland
1,705 pounds

Answer the following questions, using the information
shown above. Try to do some of the problems mentally.
Show your written work on another sheet of paper.

1. A fisherman caught a hammerhead shark and a
   sandbar shark. What is the combined weight?

2. Some newspapers reported that a great white shark
   with a weight of 7,032 pounds was caught off the
   coast of Cuba in 1945. Some scientists, however, think
   that the story is just a fish tale. What is the difference
   between the weight of the legendary Cuban great
   white shark and the weight of a typical great
   white shark?

Shark Attack! (page 2 of 2)

3. A great white shark can eat as much as 400 pounds in one meal! If a great white shark has a 352-pound dinner, what does the shark weigh immediately after finishing its meal?

4. Three 180-pound men are fishing for sharks. Which of these is a heavier load on their boat:

3 men, a Greenland shark, and a sandbar shark?

or

3 men, 2 hammerhead sharks, and a tiger shark?

How did you get your answer?

Polished Spiral Karin Kuhlmann

"Although the creation of fractals is bounded to strict mathematical rules, the results
are always very inspiring."– **Karin Kuhlmann**

Investigations

IN NUMBER, DATA, AND SPACE®

Fraction Cards and Decimal Squares

Investigation 3

Fraction Cards and Decimal Squares

4 × 6 Rectangles

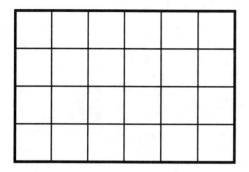
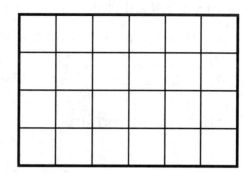

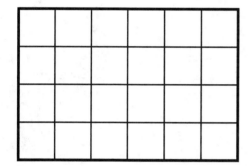
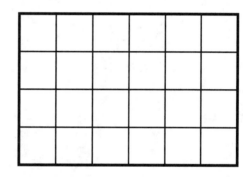

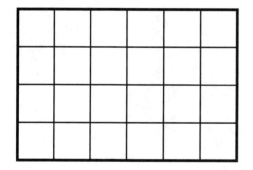
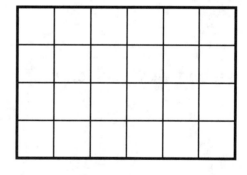

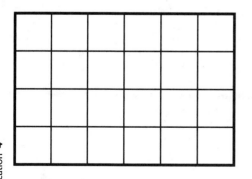
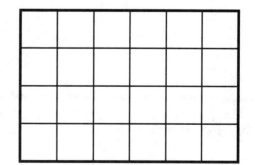

Solve Two Ways, Addition

Solve this problem in two different ways.
Be sure to show how you got your answer.

$293 + 851 =$ _____

Here is the first way I solved it:

NOTE Students practice strategies for solving addition problems in two different ways.

SMH **8–9**

Here is the second way I solved it:

Ongoing Review

$924 + 150 =$ _____

A. 1,024   **B.** 1,074   **C.** 1,390   **D.** 1,740

Halves, Fourths, and Eighths

Shade in each fraction on one of the rectangles.
Label the fraction on each rectangle.

NOTE Students represent fractions on a 4 × 6 rectangle.

SMH 53, 54, 56

$\dfrac{1}{4}$ $\dfrac{1}{2}$ $\dfrac{2}{2}$ $\dfrac{3}{4}$ $\dfrac{1}{8}$ $\dfrac{7}{8}$

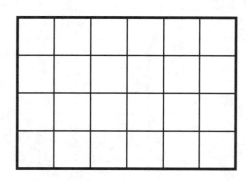

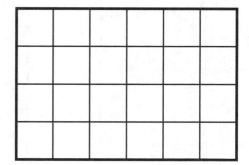

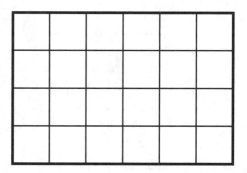

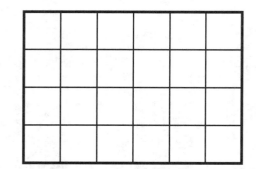

Fraction Cards and Decimal Squares

Parts of Rectangles

What fraction of the rectangle is shaded?
Write the fraction next to each figure.

NOTE Students identify fractional parts of a rectangle.

 SMH 56–57

1. _____

2. _____

3. _____

4. _____

5. _____

6. _____

7. _____

8. _____

9. _____

10. _____

Fraction Cards and Decimal Squares

Story Problems About 24 (page 1 of 2)

Solve these problems and show your solutions.

1. Ethan has 24 marbles. He gives $\frac{2}{8}$ of his collection to his sister Ruby. How many marbles does Ruby get?

2. Ruby has a collection of 24 toy cars. She gives $\frac{3}{4}$ of her collection to Ethan. How many toy cars does Ethan get?

Story Problems About 24 (page 2 of 2)

Solve these problems and show your solutions.

3. **a.** Ms. Ross's class has 24 students. $\frac{2}{3}$ of her students have brown hair. The rest have blonde hair. How many students have brown hair?

   b. What fraction of the class has blonde hair and how many students is that?

4. **a.** Ms. Perez has a crate of 24 pieces of fruit. $\frac{1}{2}$ are oranges, $\frac{1}{4}$ are mangos, and $\frac{2}{8}$ are pineapples. How many oranges are there?

   b. How many mangos are there?

   c. How many pineapples are there?

Solve Two Ways, Subtraction

NOTE Students practice strategies for solving subtraction problems in two different ways.

SMH 13–15

Solve this problem in two different ways.
Be sure to show how you got your answer.

$745 - 328 =$ _____

Here is the first way I solved it:

Here is the second way I solved it:

Ongoing Review

$2,050 - 400 - 30 =$

A. 1,020   **B.** 1,520   **C.** 1,580   **D.** 1,620

Sharing 24 (page 1 of 2)

Solve these problems and explain your solutions.

NOTE Students find fractional parts of a group of objects.

 55

Mia had 24 marbles.

1. Mia gave $\frac{1}{2}$ of her 24 marbles to Shana. How many did Shana get?

2. Mia gave $\frac{1}{3}$ of her 24 marbles to David. How many did David get?

Sharing 24 (page 2 of 2)

3. Mia gave $\frac{1}{6}$ of her 24 marbles to Yama. How many did Yama get?

4. Show each fraction on the 4×6 rectangle below. Label each piece.

Fraction Cards and Decimal Squares

5 × 12 Rectangles

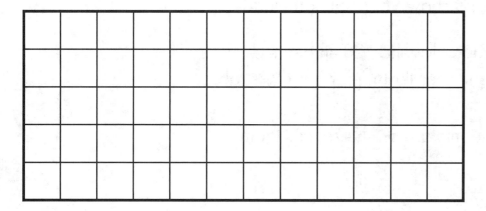

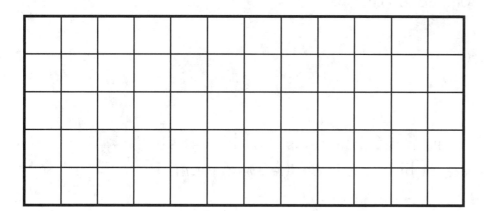

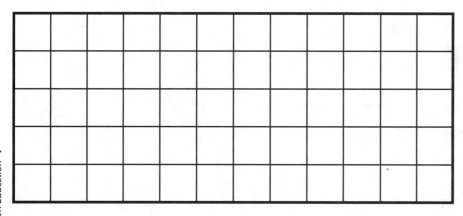

Story Problems About a Class (page 1 of 2)

Solve each problem and show your solution clearly.

1. Renata's fourth-grade class has 28 students. $\frac{1}{2}$ of her class is on the soccer team. $\frac{1}{4}$ of her class takes karate classes.

   a. How many students are on the soccer team?

   b. How many students take karate?

2. Kenji's fourth-grade class has 32 students. $\frac{1}{2}$ of his class is in the school play. $\frac{1}{4}$ of his class is on the swim team.

   a. How many students are in the play?

   b. How many students are on the swim team?

Story Problems About a Class (page 2 of 2)

Solve each problem and show your solution clearly.

3. The school play includes 60 students. $\frac{3}{5}$ of the students are actors. The rest of the students work behind the scenes.

   a. How many students act in the play?

   b. How many students work behind the scenes?

4. Luisa has 24 students in her class. $\frac{3}{4}$ of the students speak Spanish as well as English. How many students speak both Spanish and English?

5. Nick's class has 30 students. $\frac{2}{5}$ of his class sings in the school chorus. How many students sing in the chorus?

Name _____ Date _____

Fractional Parts of Groups

NOTE Students identify fractional parts of a group.

SMH 55

Solve these problems and explain your solutions.

1. Logan caught 16 butterflies this morning. By the evening, $\frac{1}{4}$ of the butterflies had flown away. How many butterflies remain?

2. Talisha collected pledges from 40 people for the charity race. $\frac{1}{8}$ of the people are family members. How many people who pledged are family members?

3. Paul hit 33 tennis balls during practice. He hit $\frac{1}{3}$ of them out of the tennis court. How many balls did he hit out of the court?

4. Maria read 90 books last school year. She read $\frac{2}{3}$ of the books before spring break. How many books did she read before spring break last year?

© Pearson Education 4

Finding Fractions of a Number

Solve these problems and show your solutions.

> **NOTE** Students find fractional parts of different numbers.
>
> **SMH** 55

1. **a.** What is $\frac{1}{2}$ of 24? **b.** What is $\frac{1}{3}$ of 24? **c.** What is $\frac{1}{4}$ of 24?

2. **a.** What is $\frac{1}{2}$ of 30? **b.** What is $\frac{1}{3}$ of 30? **c.** What is $\frac{2}{3}$ of 30?

3. **a.** What is $\frac{1}{2}$ of 60? **b.** What is $\frac{1}{3}$ of 60? **c.** What is $\frac{1}{4}$ of 60?

4. Show with a diagram or picture why $\frac{1}{2}$ of 60 is not the same as $\frac{1}{2}$ of 24.

Fraction Cards and Decimal Squares

Addition and Subtraction Problems

> **NOTE** Students practice solving addition and subtraction problems.
>
> SMH **8–9, 13–15**

Solve the problems below. Show your solutions using clear and concise notation.

1.
$$\begin{array}{r} 738 \\ -680 \\ \hline \end{array}$$

2.
$$\begin{array}{r} 515 \\ -472 \\ \hline \end{array}$$

3. $811 + 749 =$ _____

4.
$$\begin{array}{r} 1{,}234 \\ +\ 694 \\ \hline \end{array}$$

5. _____ $+ 349 = 1{,}250$

6. $865 -$ _____ $= 347$

Show the Fraction

Use these rectangles to show the following fractions as clearly as you can. Explain your thinking about each one.

NOTE Students represent fractional parts of a rectangle.

 56–57

1. $\frac{5}{6}$

2. $\frac{3}{3}$

3. $\frac{4}{8}$

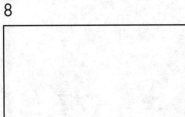

4. $\frac{2}{3}$

Adding Fractions (page 1 of 3)

Solve each problem and show your solution.

1. Alexa ate $\frac{1}{8}$ of a sandwich. Dwayne ate another $\frac{1}{8}$ of the same sandwich. Sara ate $\frac{1}{4}$ of the same sandwich.

   a. How much of the sandwich did Alexa, Dwayne, and Sara eat altogether?

   b. What fraction of the sandwich is left?

2. Ms. Russell has 24 students in her class. $\frac{3}{8}$ of the class went out for recess. $\frac{1}{4}$ went to the library. The rest stayed in the classroom.

   a. What fraction of the class was out of the classroom?

   b. How many students is that?

Fraction Cards and Decimal Squares

Adding Fractions (page 2 of 3)

Solve each problem and show your solution.

3. $\frac{1}{2} + \frac{3}{8} =$ _____

4. $\frac{1}{3} + \frac{1}{2} + \frac{2}{3} =$ _____

5. $\frac{1}{2} + \frac{3}{6} + \frac{4}{8} =$ _____

6. $\frac{5}{6} + \frac{1}{3} =$ _____

7. $\frac{3}{12} + \frac{1}{2} + \frac{1}{4} =$ _____

8. $\frac{1}{4} + \frac{3}{8} + \frac{1}{4} =$ _____

Adding Fractions (page 3 of 3)

Solve each problem and show your solution.

9. Leon bought a big bag of marbles. $\frac{1}{3}$ of them are blue. $\frac{1}{6}$ of them are red. The rest are yellow.

   a. What fraction of the marbles is yellow?

   b. There were 30 marbles in the bag. Arielle borrowed the blue and red marbles. How many marbles did she borrow?

10. Write fractions to show all the parts of this rectangle. Then write an equation that shows how all the fractional parts add up to 1.

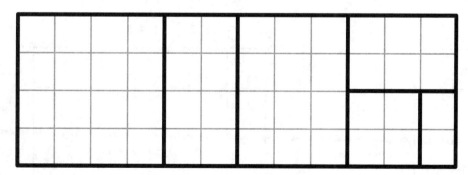

_____ + _____ + _____ + _____ + _____ + _____ = 1

Fraction Cards and Decimal Squares

Combinations That Equal 1

Use these rectangles to find combinations of fractions that equal 1. Show the fractions on each rectangle and write the matching equation underneath.

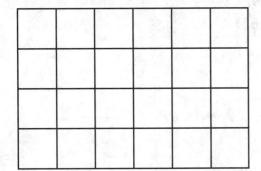

_____ = 1

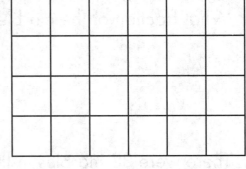

_____ = 1

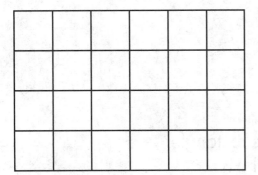

_____ = 1

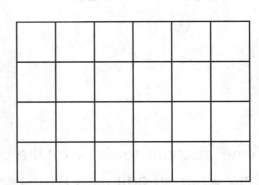

_____ = 1

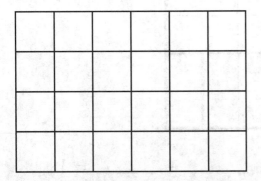

_____ = 1

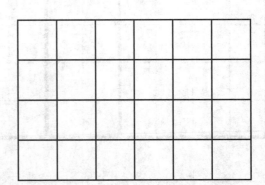

_____ = 1

10 × 10 Squares

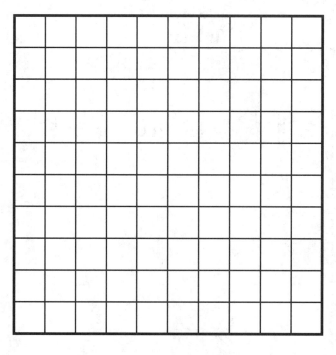

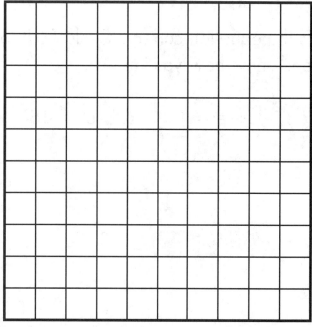

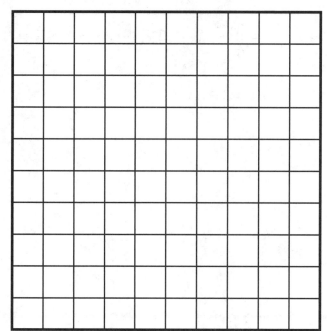

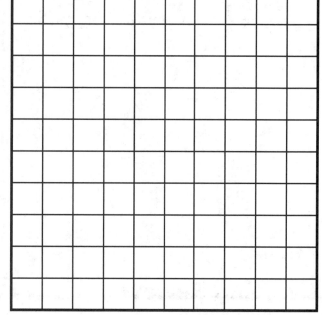

Sums of Fractions That Equal 1: True or False?

Is the equation correct? Circle TRUE or FALSE and show how you know.

> **NOTE** Students decide whether an equation involving fractions is true or false.
>
> SMH 62

1. $\frac{1}{3} + \frac{2}{3} = 1$ TRUE or FALSE

2. $\frac{4}{8} + \frac{3}{6} = 1$ TRUE or FALSE

3. $\frac{3}{6} + \frac{1}{3} = 1$ TRUE or FALSE

4. $\frac{2}{3} + \frac{3}{6} = 1$ TRUE or FALSE

Ongoing Review

5. Which picture does **not** show $\frac{1}{6}$ of a rectangle shaded?

A.    **B.** 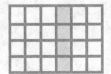   **C.** 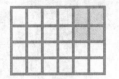   **D.**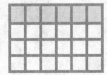

Fraction Match-Ups

Draw a line connecting each diagram to its matching fraction.

NOTE Students have been drawing diagrams to represent fractions. Ask students whether they can think of a different way to write the fraction for the diagrams in Problems 2, 3, 4, 5, and 6.

SMH 56, 57, 58

1. $\dfrac{6}{6}$

2. 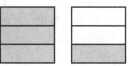 $\dfrac{8}{12}$

3. $\dfrac{3}{4}$

4. $\dfrac{12}{8}$

5. $\dfrac{4}{3}$

6. $\dfrac{5}{2}$

Ongoing Review

7. $130 - 73 =$ _____

   A. 67   **B.** 63   **C.** 57   **D.** 53

How to Make Fraction Cards

Materials for One Deck:
- 10 pieces of $8\frac{1}{2} \times 11$ inch colored oak tag or card stock, cut in fourths to make 40 cards
- *Student Activity Book* page 27, Fractions for Fraction Cards
- M16, Blank Wholes for Fraction Cards
- M17, Blank Thirds for Fraction Cards
- M18, Blank Fifths for Fraction Cards
- Scissors; glue sticks; rulers; colored pencils or crayons

Making the Cards:
1. Choose a fraction from the list of Fractions for Fraction Cards.

2. Write your fraction on a blank Fraction Card.

3. Use any of the "blanks" (blank wholes, blank thirds, or blank fifths) to make a picture for this fraction.

4. Cut out and glue your picture onto your Fraction Card above the name of the fraction. Your finished cards will look like this:

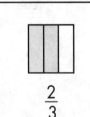

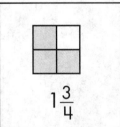

Fractions for Fraction Cards

$1\frac{3}{4}$	$\frac{1}{2}$	$1\frac{1}{2}$	$1\frac{1}{3}$
$\frac{4}{5}$	$1\frac{1}{4}$	$\frac{6}{8}$	$\frac{3}{6}$
$\frac{5}{3}$	$\frac{2}{4}$	$\frac{2}{6}$	$\frac{0}{4}$
$\frac{9}{4}$	$\frac{8}{6}$	$\frac{1}{4}$	$\frac{5}{4}$
$\frac{5}{6}$	$\frac{2}{5}$	$\frac{3}{12}$	$\frac{6}{3}$
$\frac{7}{8}$	$\frac{4}{10}$	$\frac{1}{5}$	$\frac{8}{12}$
$\frac{0}{2}$	$2\frac{1}{2}$	$\frac{8}{8}$	$\frac{3}{2}$
$\frac{2}{12}$	$\frac{1}{3}$	$\frac{9}{6}$	$\frac{2}{3}$
$\frac{1}{6}$	$\frac{3}{3}$	$\frac{4}{2}$	$\frac{1}{8}$
$\frac{5}{2}$	$\frac{3}{8}$	$\frac{3}{4}$	$\frac{4}{3}$

How Many Miles?

NOTE Students use addition and subtraction to solve problems about distances in miles.

 13–15

The Kwan family is taking a trip across the United States. They started in New York, will drive to California, and then drive back. Solve the following problems about their mileage and explain how you found the difference between the numbers.

1. On July 1, they have gone 425 miles. How many more miles until they have gone 1,000 miles?

2. On July 5, they have gone 620 miles. How many more miles until they have gone 2,000 miles?

3. On July 20, they have gone 1,495 miles. How many more miles until they have gone 3,000 miles?

4. On August 1, they are about halfway back to New York. They have gone 4,690 miles. Their total trip will be about 6,000 miles. How many more miles do they still have to drive?

Ongoing Review

5. $5,010 - \underline{\hspace{2cm}} = 4,880$

   A. 30   **B.** 50   **C.** 130   **D.** 220

Fraction Cards and Decimal Squares

Combinations That Equal 1

Fill in the blanks to make each equation true. You may want to use the grids to help you model each problem.

NOTE Students find combinations of fractions with different denominators that equal 1. They use a 10 × 10 grid to model their work.

SMH 59, 62

1. $\frac{1}{2} + \frac{1}{8} +$ _____ $= 1$

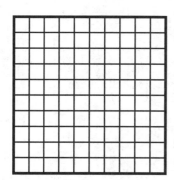

2. $\frac{2}{8} + \frac{1}{4} +$ _____ $= 1$

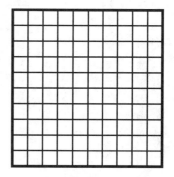

3. $\frac{1}{4} + \frac{3}{4} +$ _____ $= 1$

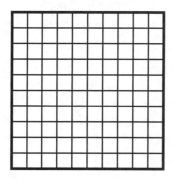

4. $\frac{2}{5} + \frac{5}{10} +$ _____ $= 1$

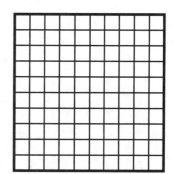

What's the Fraction?

1. Here are pictures of some Fraction Cards. On each one, write the name of the shaded fraction that is shown.

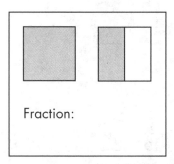

Fraction: _____

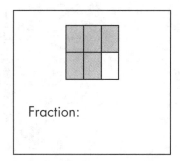

Fraction: _____

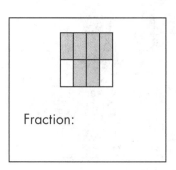

Fraction: _____

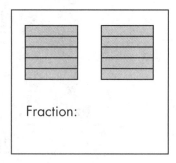

Fraction: _____

2. Choose one of the fractions above and draw a picture of an equivalent fraction.

3. How do you know these two fractions are equivalent? Write in the space below or on another sheet of paper.

Fraction Cards and Decimal Squares

Is That True?

Decide if each equation is true or false.
Write T or F.

NOTE Students determine whether an equation involving fractions is true or false.

SMH 59, 62

1. $\frac{1}{2} + \frac{1}{2} = 1$ _____

2. $\frac{1}{4} + \frac{1}{4} = \frac{1}{2}$ _____

3. $\frac{2}{4} = \frac{1}{2}$ _____

4. $\frac{1}{8} + \frac{1}{8} = \frac{1}{16}$ _____

5. $\frac{1}{4} + \frac{1}{4} + \frac{1}{4} + \frac{1}{4} = 1$ _____

6. $\frac{1}{2} + \frac{1}{4} + \frac{1}{8} + \frac{1}{16} = 1$ _____

7. $\frac{1}{16} + \frac{1}{16} = \frac{1}{8}$ _____

8. $\frac{1}{4} + \frac{1}{8} + \frac{1}{8} = \frac{1}{2}$ _____

9. $\frac{4}{8} = \frac{1}{4}$ _____

10. $\frac{2}{4} = \frac{4}{8}$ _____

Ongoing Review

11. If you take an elevator from the second floor below ground level to the 18th floor, how many floors have you traveled?

   A. 36   **B.** 22   **C.** 20   **D.** 16

Finding Equivalent Fractions

As you are playing *Capture Fractions,* keep track of the matches you make by writing equations that show equivalent fractions.

Example: $\frac{1}{2} = \frac{4}{8}$

I found these equivalent fractions:

Reading a Long Book

Solve these problems. Show your work.

NOTE Students practice solving addition and subtraction problems in a story problem context.

SMH 8–9, 13–15

1. Ravi is reading a book that is 1,200 pages long. So far, he has read 189 pages. How many more pages does he have to read to finish the book?

2. Over the next three weeks, Ravi reads 342 more pages. How many pages has he read so far?

3. At the end of six weeks, Ravi has read 977 pages. How many more pages does he have left to finish the book?

Ongoing Review

4. How many tens are there in 3,102?

   A. 31   **B.** 310   **C.** 3,100   **D.** 3,102

Which Is Larger?

Which is larger, $\frac{2}{3}$ or $\frac{3}{2}$? Use words and pictures to explain your answer.

NOTE Students compare pairs of fractions.

SMH 60–61

Fractions in Containers

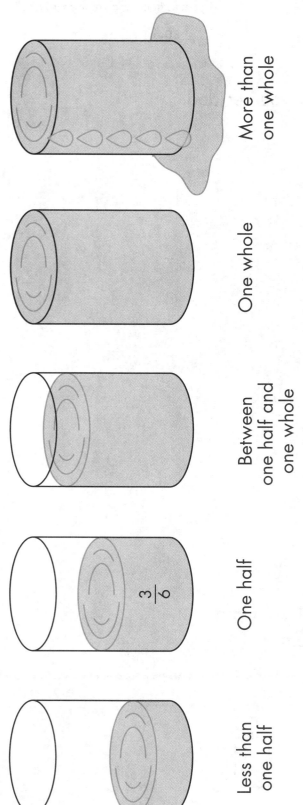

More than one whole

One whole

Between one half and one whole

One half

$\frac{3}{6}$

Less than one half

Write each fraction in the container in which it belongs.

Cross out each fraction as you use it. ($\frac{3}{6}$ has been done for you.)

There are five fractions for each container.

$\cancel{\frac{3}{6}}$ $\frac{5}{5}$ $\frac{1}{4}$ $\frac{5}{2}$ $\frac{2}{3}$ $\frac{2}{2}$ $\frac{3}{5}$ $\frac{5}{7}$ $\frac{6}{3}$ $\frac{2}{5}$ $\frac{2}{4}$ $\frac{3}{3}$

$\frac{10}{20}$ $\frac{3}{10}$ $\frac{10}{5}$ $\frac{2}{6}$ $\frac{9}{10}$ $\frac{6}{5}$ $\frac{10}{10}$ $\frac{4}{8}$ $\frac{4}{5}$ $\frac{8}{8}$ $\frac{6}{12}$

Comparing Fractions

NOTE Students decide which of two fractions is greater and put the fractions in order on a number line.

 60–61

1. Circle the larger fraction in each pair.
   Write = if you think that the fractions are equal.

   Next to each pair, show or write how you decided.

   a. $\frac{5}{8}$ $\frac{1}{2}$

   b. $\frac{3}{4}$ $\frac{7}{8}$

   c. $\frac{2}{3}$ $\frac{3}{2}$

2. Put these fractions in order from smallest to largest.
   Use the clothesline below to order them.

   $\frac{1}{2}$ $\frac{3}{8}$ $\frac{9}{5}$ $\frac{1}{6}$ $\frac{3}{2}$

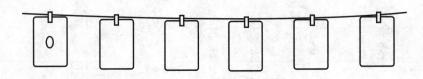

Making Fraction Number Lines

With half of your group's deck of Fraction Cards, make a number line by laying each card out in order from least to greatest. Use your Landmark Cards (0, $\frac{1}{2}$, 1, and 2) to help you. Record where you place each fraction on the number lines below.

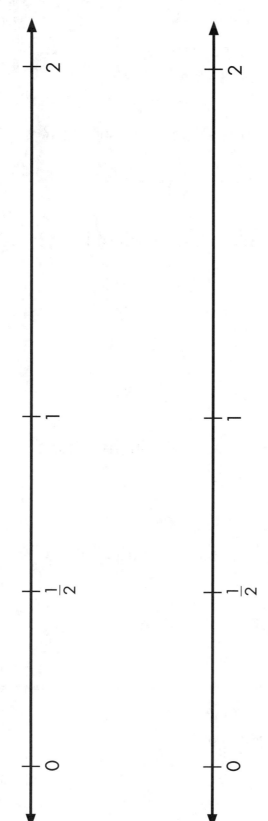

School Supplies

> **NOTE** Students practice solving addition and subtraction problems in a story problem context involving money.
>
> **SMH** 8–9, 13–15

1. Leah had $15.00 to spend on school supplies. She spent $3.75 on pencils, $2.55 on a pencil sharpener, and $5.25 on paper.

   a. How much money did she spend on supplies?

   b. After buying the supplies, how much of her $15.00 is left?

2. Diego purchases a dictionary for $12.89 and notebooks for $5.49.

   a. How much money did he spend on these supplies?

   b. If he pays $20.00, how much change will he receive?

Ongoing Review

3. Which fraction is equal to $\frac{1}{8}$?

   A. $\frac{2}{18}$ **B.** $\frac{2}{4}$ **C.** $\frac{8}{16}$ **D.** $\frac{2}{16}$

More or Less Than 1?

Fill in $<$, $>$, or $=$ to make each equation true.

NOTE Students find combinations of fractions that equal 1 and decide which of two fractions is greater. Students can use the 10 × 10 squares to help them think through their ideas about fractional parts of wholes.

SMH 60–62

1. $\dfrac{1}{4} + \dfrac{2}{4}$ _____ 1

2. 1 _____ $\dfrac{1}{2} + \dfrac{1}{4} + \dfrac{1}{8} + \dfrac{1}{16}$

3. $\dfrac{2}{3} + \dfrac{2}{3}$ _____ 1

4. $\dfrac{3}{4}$ _____ $\dfrac{4}{5}$

5. $\dfrac{1}{2} + \dfrac{5}{5}$ _____ 1

Write fractions in the blanks to make each equation true.

6. _____ + _____ $>$ 1

7. _____ + _____ $<$ 1

8. _____ + _____ $=$ 1

42 Unit 6

Make Your Move

The fractions on each clothesline are out of order.
Show how to fix the order with just one move.

NOTE Students put fractions in the correct order.

SMH **60–61**

1.
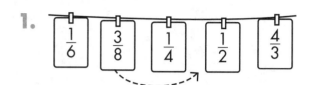

I need to move the $\frac{3}{8}$. $\frac{1}{4}$ is the same as $\frac{2}{8}$, and $\frac{1}{2}$ is the same as $\frac{4}{8}$. So $\frac{3}{8}$ should go between them.

2.
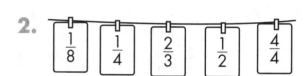

3.
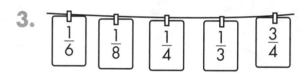

4.
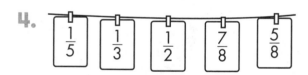

5.

Ongoing Review

6. Which total is **less than** 100?

    A. 44 + 54   **B.** 53 + 57   **C.** 81 + 20   **D.** 76 + 24

Decimal Grids (page 1 of 2)

Whole

Grid A

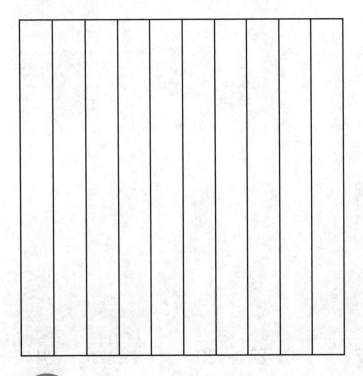

Decimal Grids (page 2 of 2)

Grid B

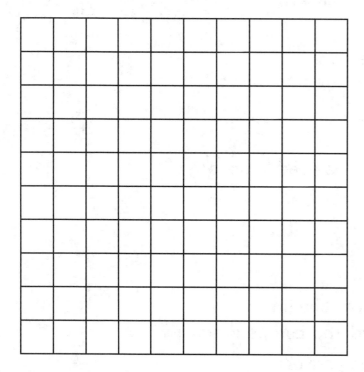

Grid C

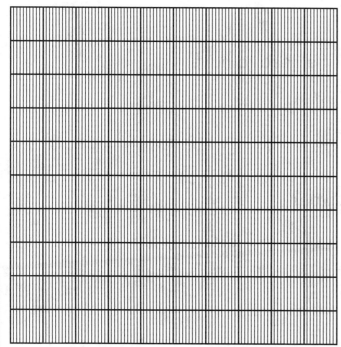

Stamp Collection

NOTE Students practice solving addition and subtraction problems in a story problem context.

SMH 8–9, 13–15

1. José has a collection of stamps. He has 399 stamps from North America and 218 stamps from South America.

   a. How many stamps does José have?

   b. How many more stamps does he need to have 800 altogether?

2. Aliyah also has a stamp collection. She has 441 North American stamps and 183 European stamps.

   a. How many stamps does Aliyah have?

   b. How many more stamps does she need to have 800 altogether?

3. Who has more stamps, José or Aliyah? By how many stamps?

Everyday Uses of Fractions and Decimals

Look for everyday uses of fractions and decimals. List what you find below. Try looking in the newspaper, in your cupboards, and all around your home.

NOTE Students learn about decimals and how they relate to fractions. At home, they will look for examples of how fractions and decimals are used in the real world.

SMH **53, 64**

Everyday uses of fractions:

Everyday uses of decimals:

Daily Practice

Selling Fruit

NOTE Students practice solving addition and subtraction problems in a story problem context.

SMH **8–9, 13–15**

1. On Monday, a grocery store received a shipment of 700 peaches. The store sold 567 of them that day. How many peaches were left to sell the next day?

2. On Wednesday, the store received a shipment of 850 grapefruits. The store sold 362 grapefruits that day. How many grapefruits were left to sell the next day?

3. On Saturday, the store received a shipment of 1,500 melons. The store sold 734 melons on Saturday and 674 melons on Sunday.

   a. How many melons did they sell on the weekend (Saturday and Sunday)?

   b. How many melons were left to sell on Monday morning?

Ongoing Review

4. Which number is "three tenths"?

   A. 0.03　　**B.** 0.3　　**C.** 3.0　　**D.** 3.10

Name _____   Date _____

Showing Decimals on a 10 × 10 Square

NOTE Students shade in decimal numbers on a square that represents 1.

 65–68

Show the following decimal numbers on the squares below by shading in each amount. Each square represents 1.

0.7

1.

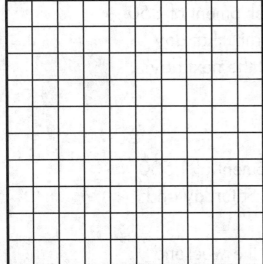

0.75

2.

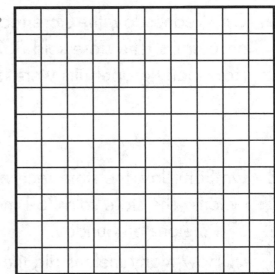

0.5

3.

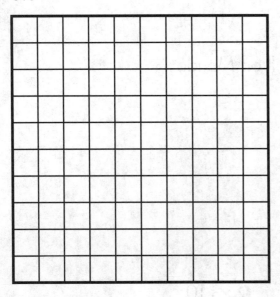

0.38

4.

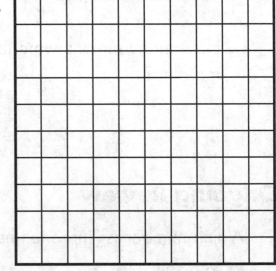

© Pearson Education 4

Daily Practice

More Showing Decimals on a 10 × 10 Square

NOTE Students represent decimals on a square that represents 1.

SMH 65

Show the following decimal numbers on the squares below by shading in each amount. Each square represents 1.

0.1

1.

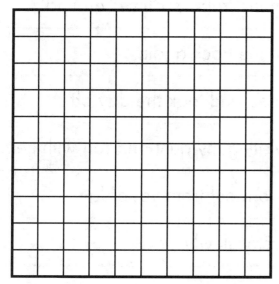

0.45

2.

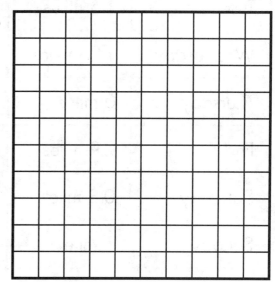

0.6

3.

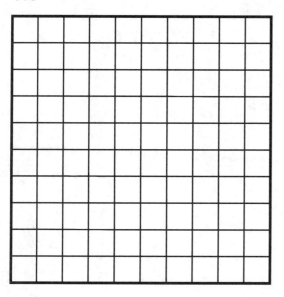

0.95

4.

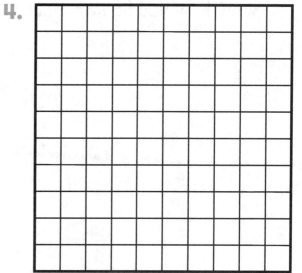

Fraction Cards and Decimal Squares

Runner's Log (page 1 of 2)

Tony made a log of how many miles he ran during
a week.

Day	Mileage	Comments
Monday	2.2 miles	I ran around the pond once.
Tuesday	1.5 miles	I ran on the track, six times around.
Wednesday	1.25 miles	I ran on the track again.
Thursday	0 miles	I was tired and took the day off.
Friday	2.9 miles	I was visiting my aunt and ran with her.
Saturday	0.8 mile	I was worn out from yesterday.
Sunday	1 mile	I ran pretty slowly.

1. How far did Tony run this week? _____

2. Show how you figured it out.

Fraction Cards and Decimal Squares

Runner's Log (page 2 of 2)

Dana: $9\frac{1}{2}$ years old; has run two races before

Day	Mileage	Comments
Monday	1.75 miles	I ran with my mom to the store, but we got a ride back.
Tuesday	1.6 miles	Jamie and I ran to school because we were late!
Wednesday	0 miles	I had to babysit today, so I could not run.
Thursday	3.2 miles	I ran slowly, but much farther than before.
Friday	0.5 miles	I was really tired, so I only ran around the track twice.
Saturday	1.75 miles	I ran home from the store, but slowly.
Sunday	0.8 mile	I ran pretty fast, but not very far.

3. How many miles did Dana run? _____

4. Show how you figured it out.

Coin Jars

NOTE Students solve problems about combinations of coins.

 70–71

1. Quincy has a coin jar full of pennies, dimes, nickels, and quarters. He knows that there is $4.50 in his coin jar. What combination of coins could be in Quincy's coin jar that would equal $4.50?

   First solution: Second solution:

2. Petra also has a coin jar. There are only two kinds of coins in her coin jar. She knows that there is $3.90 in her jar. What combination of coins could be in Petra's coin jar that would equal $3.90?

   First solution: Second solution:

Ongoing Review

3. Which number is less than 0.5?

   A. 0.05   **B.** 0.55   **C.** .5   **D.** 0.50

Which Is More?

Circle the decimal that is a larger amount. Explain how you figured out which is more.

NOTE Students work with and compare some common decimals in order to decide which number is larger.

SMH 69

1.   0.5   or   0.45

2.   0.10   or   0.01

3.   0.5   or   0.50

Make a Running Log (page 1 of 2)

Make an imaginary running log. Fill in the mileage for each day. Make sure that your total mileage for the week is 10.5.

Log 1: Each distance must include tenths or hundredths.

Day	Mileage	Comments

How did you make the miles add up to 10.5?
How did you think about this problem?

Make a Running Log (page 2 of 2)

Make an imaginary running log. Fill in the mileage for each day. Make sure that your total mileage for the week is 10.5.

Log 2: Day 1 is 2.3 miles and Day 5 is 1.7 miles.

Fill in the rest to make a total of 10.5 miles.

Day	Mileage	Comments
1	2.3 miles	
5	1.7 miles	

How did you make the miles add up to 10.5?
How did you think about this problem?

Daily Practice

Comparing Fractions 2

Circle the greater fraction.

NOTE Students determine which is the greater fraction in each pair.

SMH 60–61

1. $\frac{1}{3}$ $\frac{3}{5}$

2. $\frac{5}{6}$ $\frac{2}{3}$

3. $\frac{1}{2}$ $\frac{1}{8}$

4. $\frac{3}{10}$ $\frac{3}{5}$

5. $\frac{4}{5}$ $\frac{1}{2}$

6. $\frac{7}{10}$ $\frac{1}{4}$

7. $\frac{3}{8}$ $\frac{5}{8}$

8. $\frac{2}{3}$ $\frac{3}{4}$

9. $\frac{1}{4}$ $\frac{3}{8}$

10. $\frac{4}{8}$ $\frac{3}{5}$

11. $\frac{9}{10}$ $\frac{4}{5}$

12. $\frac{2}{8}$ $\frac{1}{3}$

Ongoing Review

13. Which shows the fractions in order from least to greatest?

     A. $\frac{1}{2}, \frac{3}{8}, \frac{1}{6}$ **C.** $\frac{3}{8}, \frac{1}{2}, \frac{1}{6}$

     B. $\frac{1}{6}, \frac{3}{8}, \frac{1}{2}$ **D.** $\frac{1}{6}, \frac{1}{2}, \frac{3}{8}$

How Many Hundreds?
How Many Altogether?

NOTE Students estimate and solve addition problems.

 SMH 8–9

Number of Postcards in Six Collections	About how many hundreds altogether? Estimate.	Add the numbers to find the exact total.
61 14 52 39 59 98	100 or 200 or 300 or 400? How did you decide?	

Cost of Four Items at the Grocery Store	About how many dollars altogether? Estimate.	Add the numbers to find the exact total.
$0.91 $2.41 $1.77 $3.04	$6.00 or $7.00 or $8.00 or $9.00 How did you decide?	

Fraction Cards and Decimal Squares

Summer Sale!

Belinda's Toys and Hobby Shop is having a summer sale. Here are some of the sale items.

NOTE Students calculate and compare fractional parts of groups.

SMH 55

1. Calculate the sale prices.

$\frac{1}{4}$ off a stuffed animal _____ $\frac{1}{3}$ off a book _____
You saved $_____   *You saved* $_____

$\frac{1}{2}$ off a puzzle _____ $\frac{1}{5}$ off a board game _____
You saved $_____   *You saved* $_____

2. Which discount is greater?

a. $\frac{1}{3}$ off 2 stuffed animals or $\frac{1}{4}$ off 4 books _____
Explain your thinking.

b. $\frac{1}{3}$ off a puzzle or $\frac{1}{3}$ off 3 books _____
Explain your thinking.

Polished Spiral Karin Kuhlmann

"Although the creation of fractals is bounded to strict mathematical rules, the results are always very inspiring."– **Karin Kuhlmann**

Investigations

IN NUMBER, DATA, AND SPACE®

Moving Between Solids and Silhouettes

Geometric Solids

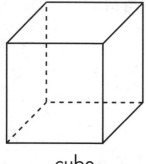

cube

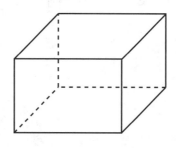

rectangular prism

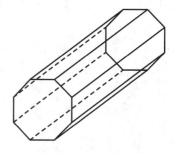

octagonal prism

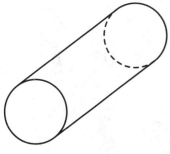

cylinder

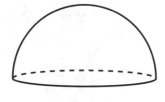

hemisphere

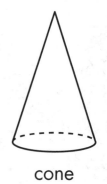

cone

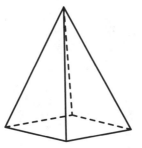

hexagonal prism

square pyramid

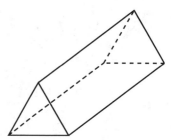

triangular prism

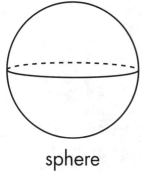

sphere

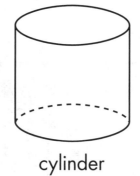

cylinder

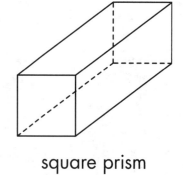

square prism

Daily Practice

Comparing Decimals

Fill in <, >, or = to make each expression true.

NOTE Students compare the sizes of different decimals.

 69

1. 0.15 _____ 1.5

2. 0.05 _____ 0.5

3. 0.3 _____ 0.25

4. 0.95 _____ 0.9

5. 0.60 _____ 0.6

6. 0.85 _____ 0.05

7. 0.55 _____ 0.01

8. 0.95 _____ 1.0

Sharing 60

NOTE Students find fractions of a group of objects.

SMH 62

Solve these problems and explain your solutions.

There are 60 milk cartons in a crate.

1. Mr. Daniel's class took $\frac{1}{2}$ of the milk cartons in the crate. How many milk cartons did they take?

2. Ms. Kim's class took $\frac{1}{6}$ of the milk cartons in the crate. How many milk cartons did they take?

3. Ms. Glasgow's class took $\frac{1}{5}$ of the milk cartons in the crate. How many milk cartons did they take?

4. Show each fraction on the 5×12 grid below. Label each piece.

Silhouettes of Geometric Solids

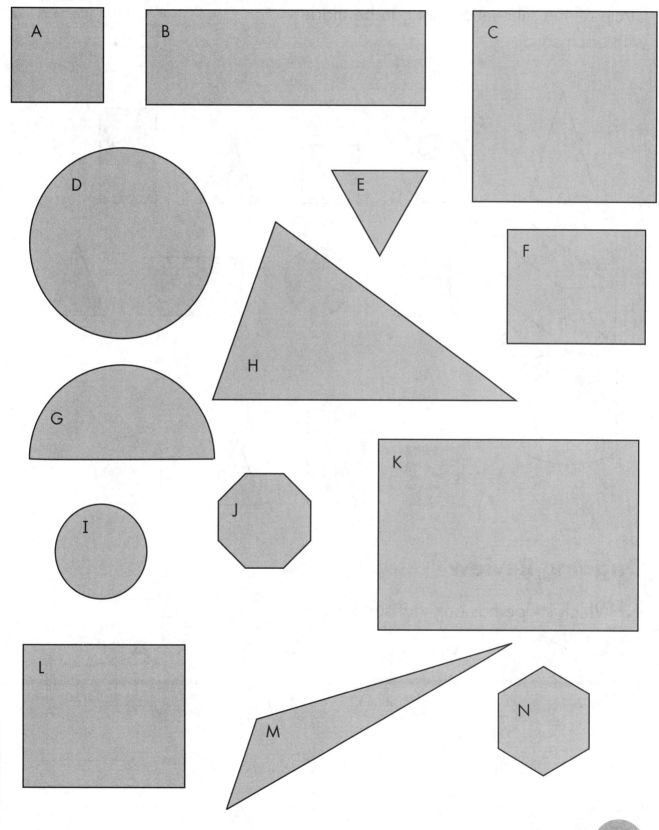

Don't Block My Shadow

Circle all the silhouettes that can be made with each solid.

NOTE Students determine which silhouettes can be made from a given solid.

 122–123

1.

2.

3.

Ongoing Review

4. Which shape has only flat surfaces?

A.   B.   C.   D.

Session 1.2

Landscape 1

Build this landscape with your geometric solids. Then look at each pair of silhouettes below. Find all of the points in the landscape from which you could see both silhouettes in a pair. Write the letters of these points beside the silhouettes.

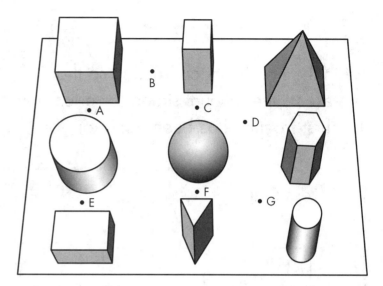

Pair 1
Points from which these could be seen:

_____

Pair 2
Points from which these could be seen:

_____

Pair 3
Points from which these could be seen:

_____

Fill-In Fractions

Fill in the box for each fraction so that it represents the amount stated for each box. The first fraction has been done for you.

NOTE Students place fractions equal to or between landmarks.

SMH 60–61

---

1. Less than $\frac{1}{2}$

$\dfrac{3}{8}$ $\dfrac{3}{\boxed{}}$ $\dfrac{\boxed{}}{5}$

2. $\frac{1}{2}$

$\dfrac{\boxed{}}{4}$ $\dfrac{5}{\boxed{}}$ $\dfrac{\boxed{}}{12}$

---

3. Between $\frac{1}{2}$ and 1

$\dfrac{2}{\boxed{}}$ $\dfrac{\boxed{}}{6}$ $\dfrac{3}{\boxed{}}$

4. 1

$\dfrac{\boxed{}}{3}$ $\dfrac{\boxed{}}{8}$ $\dfrac{2}{\boxed{}}$

---

5. Between 1 and $1\frac{1}{2}$

$\dfrac{\boxed{}}{8}$ $\dfrac{6}{\boxed{}}$ $\dfrac{5}{\boxed{}}$

6. More than $1\frac{1}{2}$

$\dfrac{5}{\boxed{}}$ $\dfrac{\boxed{}}{3}$ $\dfrac{4}{\boxed{}}$

Mystery Silhouettes

List objects you find at home that make silhouettes that are these shapes. The size of the silhouette does not have to match.

NOTE Students have been studying the silhouettes (shadows) of geometric shapes. Using a flashlight or other bright light will help students find silhouettes.

SMH 122–123

1. ⬛ Object(s) I found that make a square silhouette:

   _____

   _____

2. ▲ Object(s) I found that make a triangular silhouette:

   _____

   _____

3.  Object(s) I found that make both a rectangular silhouette and a circular silhouette:

   _____

   _____

Moving Between Solids and Silhouettes

Landscape 2

Build this landscape with your geometric solids. Then look at each pair of silhouettes below. Find all of the points in the landscape from which you could see both silhouettes in a pair. Write the letters of these points beside the silhouettes.

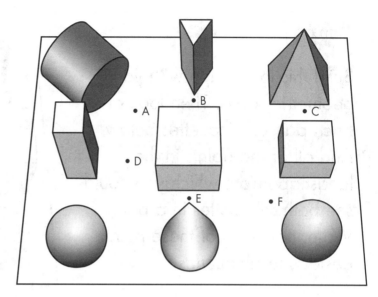

Pair 1

Points from which these could be seen:

_____

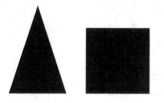

Pair 2

Points from which these could be seen:

_____

Pair 3

Points from which these could be seen:

_____

Landscape 3

Build this landscape with your geometric solids. Then look at each pair of silhouettes below. Find all of the points in the landscape from which you could see both silhouettes in a pair. Write the letters of these points beside the silhouettes.

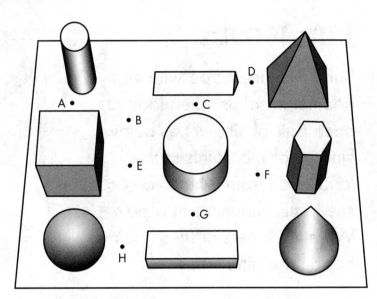

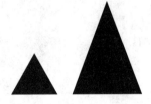

Pair 1
Points from which these could be seen:

_____

Pair 2
Points from which these could be seen:

_____

Pair 3
Points from which these could be seen:

_____

Landscape Challenge

Look at this pair of silhouettes. Find all of the points in the three geometric landscapes from which these two silhouettes could be seen. Write the letters of these points from *Student Activity Book* pages 7, 11, and 12.

These could be seen from the following points:

In Landscape 1:

_____

_____

_____

_____

In Landscape 2:

_____

_____

_____

_____

In Landscape 3:

_____

_____

_____

_____

How Many Waffles?

Solve each problem. Use pictures and words
to show how you solved each problem.

NOTE Students find the total amount
given the number of fractional parts.

 58, 62

1. Three people each get $1\frac{3}{4}$ waffles. How many waffles
   are there in all? Draw a picture and tell how many.

   _____ waffles in all

2. Draw a picture to show how four people could each
   have $2\frac{1}{3}$ waffles. Tell how many waffles in all.

   _____ waffles in all

Fractions: Which Is Bigger?

Circle the larger fraction. Explain
how you knew which fraction is larger.

NOTE Students compare the
value of different fractions.

SMH 60–61

1. $\dfrac{3}{4}$ $\dfrac{3}{2}$

2. $1\dfrac{1}{5}$ $\dfrac{3}{2}$

3. $\dfrac{2}{4}$ $\dfrac{4}{8}$

4. $\dfrac{5}{6}$ $\dfrac{6}{5}$

Moving Between Solids and Silhouettes

Make the Buildings (page 1 of 2)

1.

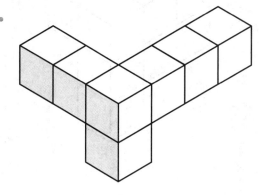

2.

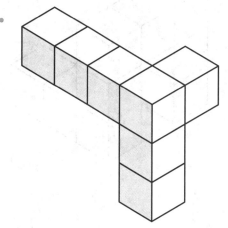

3.

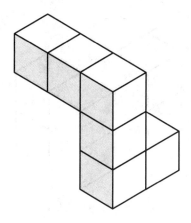

4.

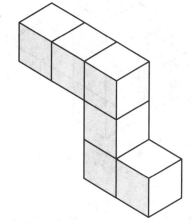

5.

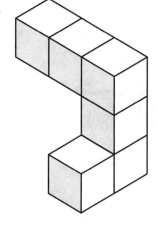

Make the Buildings (page 2 of 2)

6.

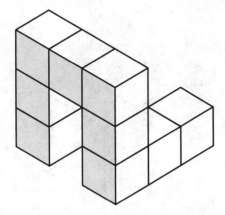

7.

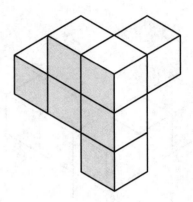

8.

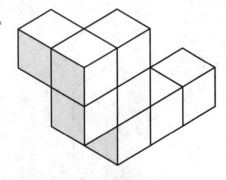

9.

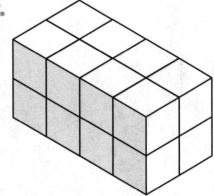

10.

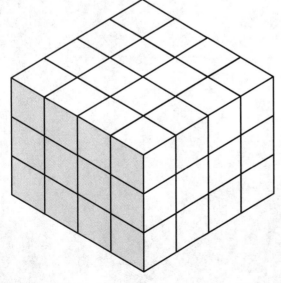

NOTE Students find fractions of a group of objects.

SMH 55

Books to Read

Solve these problems and explain your solutions.

There are 48 books on the reading list.

1. Luke read $\frac{1}{3}$ of the books on the reading list. How many books did he read?

2. Yuson read $\frac{3}{8}$ of the books on the reading list. How many books did she read?

3. Alejandro read $\frac{4}{6}$ of the books on the reading list. How many books did he read?

4. **a.** Who read the most books on the reading list?

   b. What fraction of the reading list does he or she have left to read?

How Many Cubes?

How many cubes does it take to make each building?

NOTE Student have been making cube buildings and finding the volume of these buildings.

1.

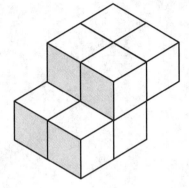

_____ cubes

2.

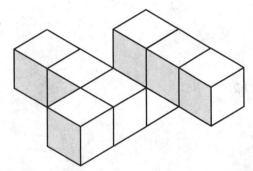

_____ cubes

3.

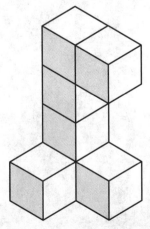

_____ cubes

Drawing Silhouettes: An Introduction

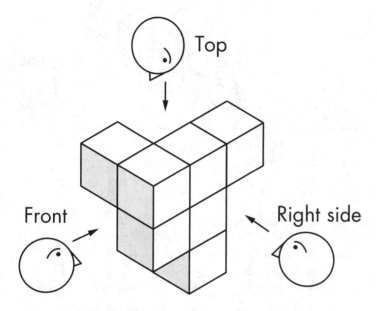

Top

Front   Right side

Use cubes to make this building.

Two silhouettes of the building are shown below.

One was seen from the front, and one was seen from the right side.

The silhouettes are drawn on graph paper so that we can see where the cubes are.

What do you think the top silhouette looks like?

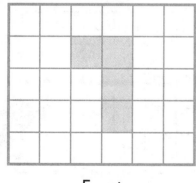

Front

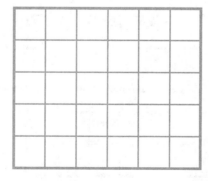

Top

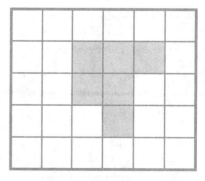

Right side

Front, Top, and Side Silhouettes (page 1 of 2)

Make each building with cubes.

Then draw the silhouettes for both.

Building 1: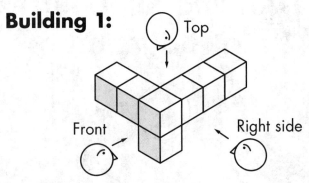

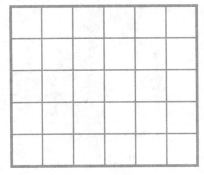

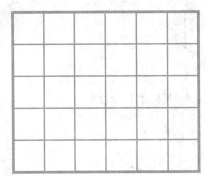

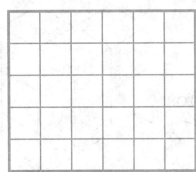

Front   Top, as seen from the front   Right side

Building 2: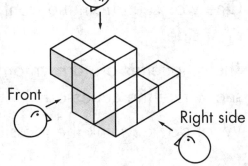

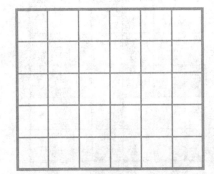

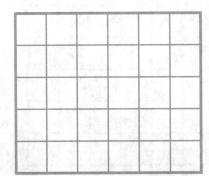

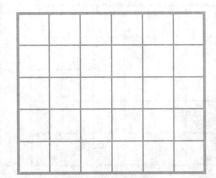

Front   Top, as seen from the front   Right side

Moving Between Solids and Silhouettes

Front, Top, and Side Silhouettes (page 2 of 2)

Make each building with cubes.

Then draw the silhouettes for both.

Building 3:

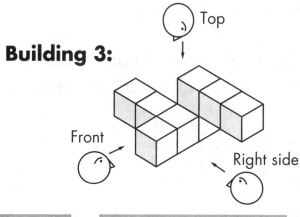

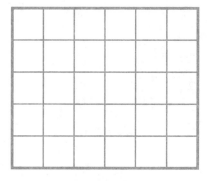

Front

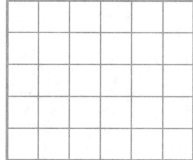

Top, as seen from the front

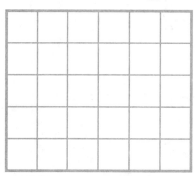

Right side

Building 4:

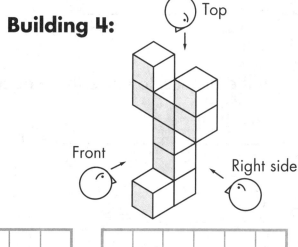

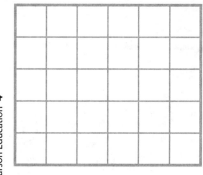

Front

Top, as seen from the front

Right side

Is That True?

NOTE Students practice adding fractions.

SMH **62**

Determine whether each equation is true or false.
Write T or F after each equation.

1. $\dfrac{2}{5} + \dfrac{1}{10} = \dfrac{1}{2}$ _____

2. $\dfrac{5}{6} = \dfrac{2}{3}$ _____

3. $\dfrac{1}{4} + \dfrac{1}{4} = \dfrac{1}{8}$ _____

4. $\dfrac{1}{8} + \dfrac{1}{8} = \dfrac{1}{4}$ _____

5. $\dfrac{1}{2} + \dfrac{1}{3} = \dfrac{4}{6}$ _____

Fill in the blank(s) to make these equations true.

6. _____ + _____ = 1

7. $\dfrac{1}{2} +$ _____ $= \dfrac{3}{4}$

8. $\dfrac{3}{5} +$ _____ $= 1\dfrac{1}{5}$

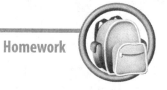

NOTE Students compare the
size of different decimals.

SMH 69

Decimals:
Which Is Bigger?

Circle the larger decimal. Explain
how you figured out each one.

1.   0.05   0.5

2.   0.33   0.2

3.   0.75   0.7

4.   1.2   2.1

Drawing Silhouettes A and B

A. Draw the three silhouettes
for this building. Do not use cubes.

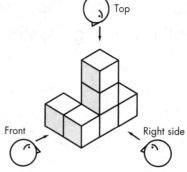

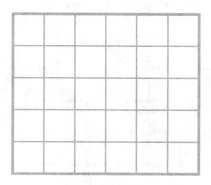 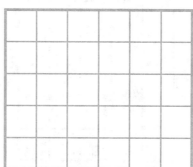 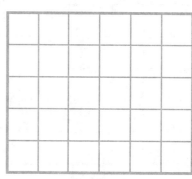

Front   Top, as seen from the front   Right side

B. Make the building with cubes.
Then draw the three silhouettes.

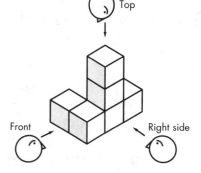

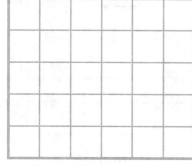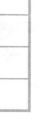 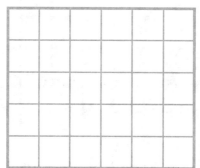 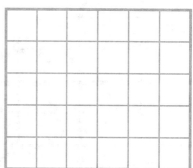

Front   Top, as seen from the front   Right side

Drawing Silhouettes C and D

C. Draw the three silhouettes
for this building. Do not use cubes.

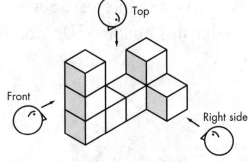

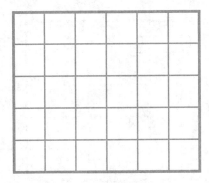

Front

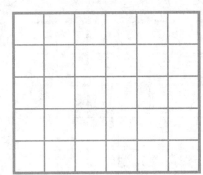

Top, as seen from the front

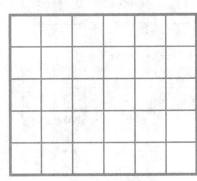

Right side

D. Make the building with cubes.
Then draw the three silhouettes.

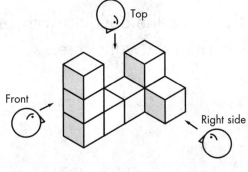

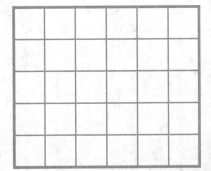

Front

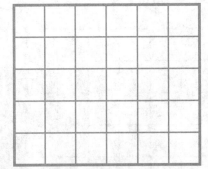

Top, as seen from the front

Right side

Name _____ Date _____

Moving Between Solids and Silhouettes

Daily Practice

Castle Builder

A student built a "castle" from blocks. Label the silhouettes below *front*, *back*, *left*, and *right*.

> **NOTE** Students explore how objects look from various perspectives.
>
> **SMH** 124

1.

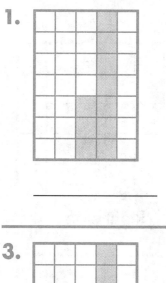

2.

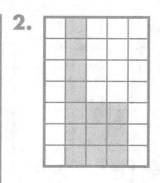

_____   _____

3.

4.

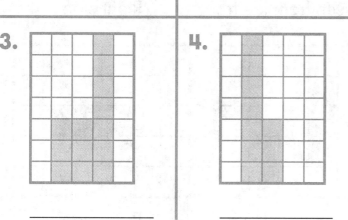

_____   _____

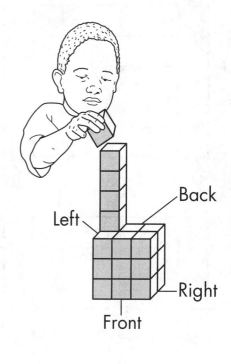

Left   Back   Right   Front

Ongoing Review

5. Choose the silhouette that is the correct one for the top of this cube building.

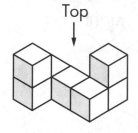

Top

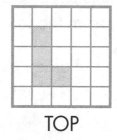

TOP

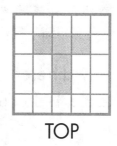

TOP

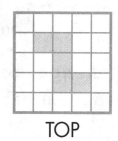

TOP

© Pearson Education 4

Session 2.3

Unit 7   **29**

Building from Silhouettes

For each puzzle below, construct a cube building that makes the three silhouettes. Do any other buildings also make these silhouettes?

1.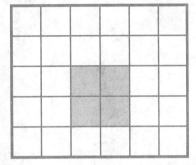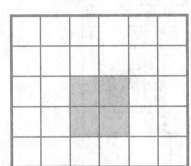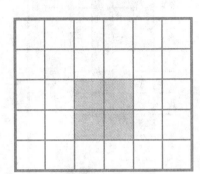

Front   Top, as seen from the front   Right side

2. 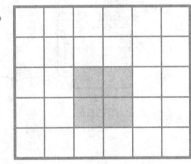 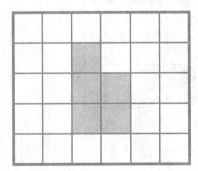

Front   Top, as seen from the front   Right side

3.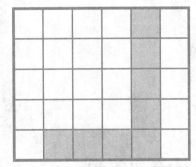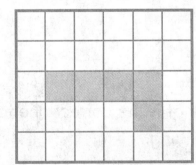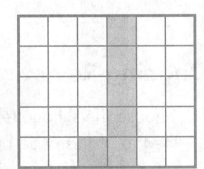

Front   Top, as seen from the front   Right side

Challenge: How many different cube buildings make three silhouettes in Puzzle 1? In Puzzle 2? In Puzzle 3?

Decimal Problems

Solve each problem by using Steve's running log below. Use another sheet of paper to solve the problems.

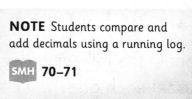

NOTE Students compare and add decimals using a running log.

SMH **70–71**

Day	Mileage	Comments
Monday	2.2 miles	I ran around the pond once.
Tuesday	1.50 miles	I ran on the track six times around.
Wednesday	1.25 miles	I ran on the track again.
Thursday	0 miles	I was tired and took a day off.
Friday	2.9 miles	I was visiting my aunt and ran with her.
Saturday	0.8 mile	I was worn out from yesterday.
Sunday	1 mile	I ran pretty slowly.

1. **a.** On what 4 days did Steve run the farthest?

   b. How many miles did he run during those 4 days?

2. **a.** On what 3 days did Steve run the shortest distance?

   b. How many miles did he run during those 3 days?

Showing Decimals on a Grid

Show the following decimals on the grids below.
Label each grid.

NOTE Students represent decimals on 10 × 10 grids.

SMH 65, 66, 67, 68

0.1   0.95   0.08   0.76

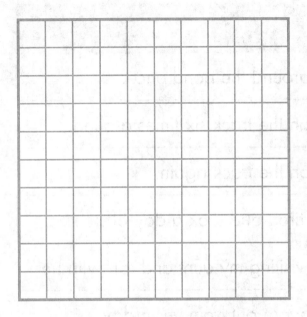 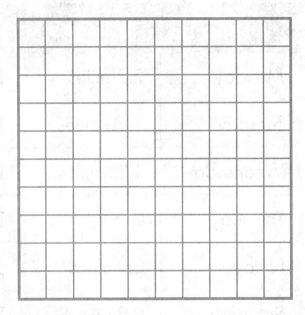

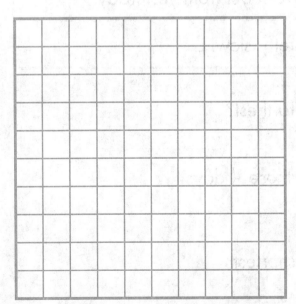 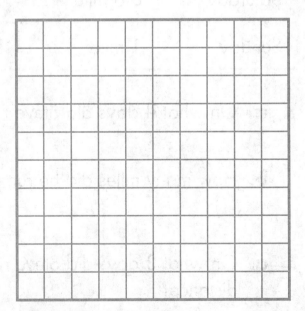

Different Views of a City

This map shows the top view of a cube city.

The eight buildings shown are made from connecting cubes.

The number on each building tells how many cubes high that building is.

A photographer flew around the city in a helicopter and took four silhouette photographs.

The photographs were taken from points A, B, C, and D (looking in the directions of the arrows).

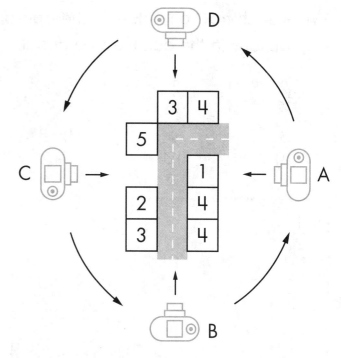

The resulting silhouettes are shown here. Below each one, write the letter of the point where it was taken.

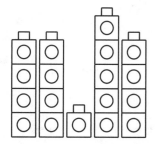 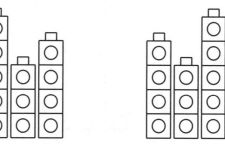 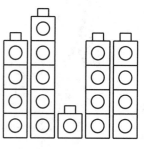

1. _____   2. _____   3. _____   4. _____

Equivalent Fractions

Write each fraction below in the appropriate box.
All fractions in the box must be equal.

NOTE Students identify equivalent fractions.

 SMH 59

$\dfrac{2}{12}$ $\qquad$ $\dfrac{2}{8}$ $\qquad$ $\dfrac{2}{4}$ $\qquad$ $\dfrac{4}{12}$ $\qquad$ $\dfrac{3}{6}$ $\qquad$ $\dfrac{3}{12}$

$\dfrac{5}{10}$ $\qquad$ $\dfrac{9}{12}$ $\qquad$ $\dfrac{4}{6}$ $\qquad$ $\dfrac{2}{6}$ $\qquad$ $\dfrac{8}{12}$ $\qquad$ $\dfrac{6}{8}$

$\dfrac{1}{2}$	$\dfrac{1}{3}$
$\dfrac{1}{4}$	$\dfrac{2}{3}$
$\dfrac{3}{4}$	$\dfrac{1}{6}$

How Many Cubes?

How many cubes fit in each box? First, determine the answer without building the box. Then build a box and use cubes to check. Compare your first answer to the actual answer before going on to the next box.

Think about a way you could determine the number of cubes that would fit in any box.

Pattern	**Picture**	**First Answer**	**Actual Answer**

Box 1 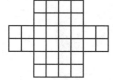 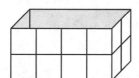 _____ _____

Box 2 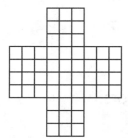 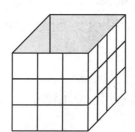 _____ _____

Box 3 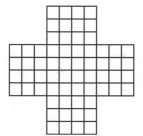 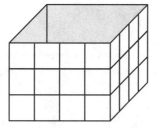 _____ _____

Fraction Story Problems

Solve each problem and show your solution.

NOTE Students solve fraction problems in a story context.

SMH 53–55, 62

1. There was a quart of milk in the refrigerator. Venetta drank $\frac{1}{4}$ of the quart. Steve drank $\frac{1}{8}$ of the quart. Kimberly drank $\frac{2}{8}$ of the quart.

   a. How much milk did Venetta, Steve, and Kimberly drink in all?

   b. How much milk is left?

2. There were 30 crackers on a plate. Lucy ate $\frac{1}{6}$ of the crackers, Abdul ate $\frac{1}{5}$ of the crackers, and Emaan ate $\frac{1}{3}$ of the crackers.

   a. Who ate the most crackers? How many crackers did he or she eat?

   b. How many crackers are left?

Comparing Decimals

Fill in <, >, or = to make each expression true.

1. 0.25 _____ 0.3

2. 0.71 _____ 0.09

3. 0.33 _____ 0.30

4. 0.02 _____ 0.17

5. 0.46 _____ 0.54

Write decimals in the blanks to make each equation true.

6. _____ + _____ > 1

7. _____ + _____ < 1

8. _____ + _____ = 1

Moving Between Solids and Silhouettes

Making Boxes from the Bottom Up (page 1 of 4)

The dark squares make the bottom of a rectangular box that contains exactly 20 cubes. The box has no top. Draw the sides to finish the pattern for the box.

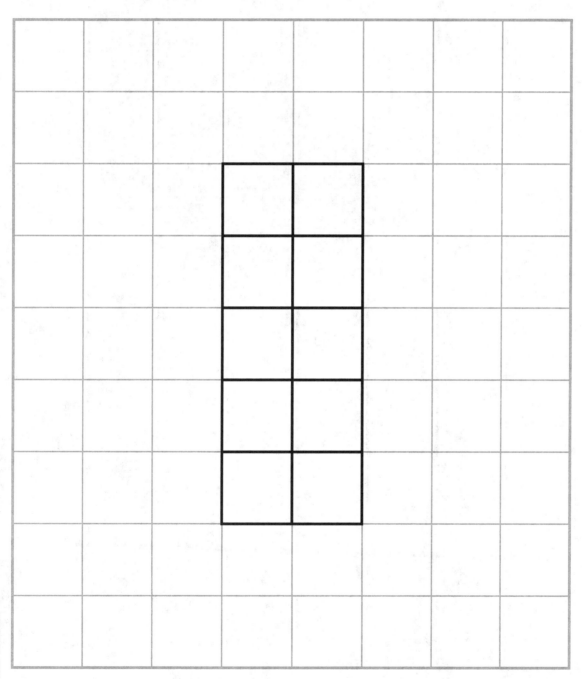

Moving Between Solids and Silhouettes

Making Boxes from the Bottom Up (page 2 of 4)

The dark squares make the bottom of a rectangular box that contains exactly 12 cubes. The box has no top. Draw the sides to finish the pattern for the box.

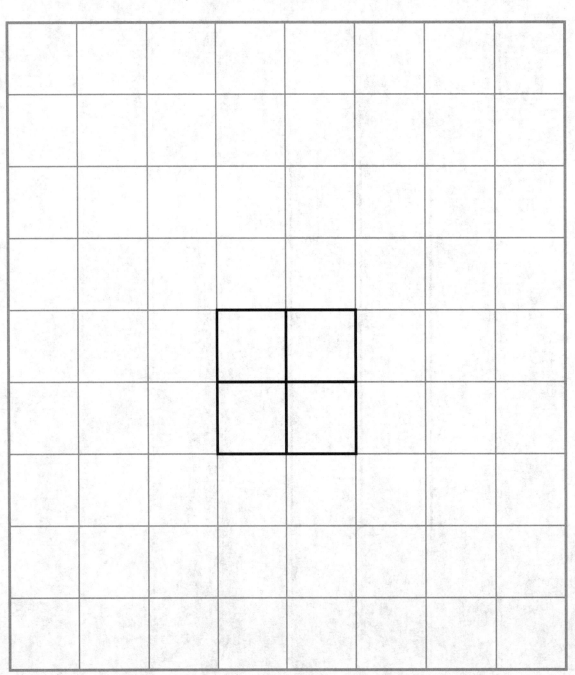

Making Boxes from the Bottom Up (page 3 of 4)

The dark squares make the bottom of a rectangular box that contains exactly 30 cubes. The box has no top. Draw the sides to finish the pattern for the box.

Making Boxes from the Bottom Up (page 4 of 4)

The dark squares make the bottom of a rectangular box that contains exactly 24 cubes. The box has no top. Draw the sides to finish the pattern for the box.

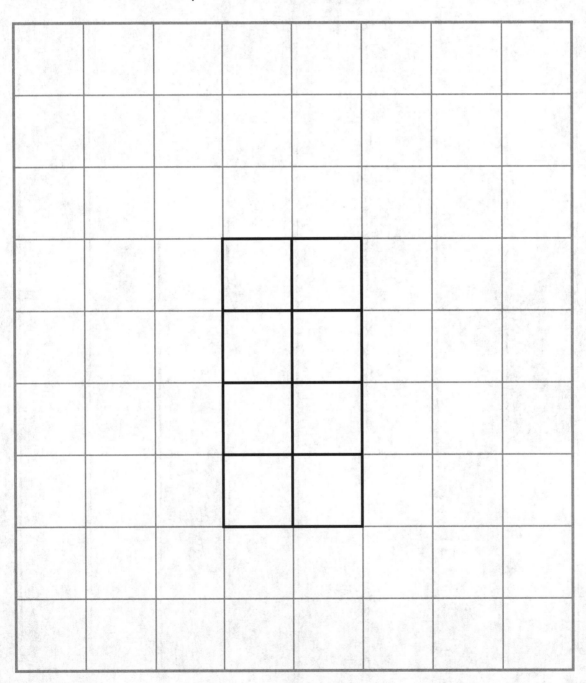

Moving Between Solids and Silhouettes

Comparing Fractions

Fill in <, >, or = to make each expression true.

> **NOTE** Students compare the value of different fractions.
> SMH **60–61**

1. $\dfrac{3}{4}$ _____ $\dfrac{4}{5}$

2. $\dfrac{7}{12}$ _____ $\dfrac{1}{2}$

3. $1\dfrac{2}{3}$ _____ $2\dfrac{1}{3}$

4. $\dfrac{5}{1}$ _____ $\dfrac{1}{5}$

5. $\dfrac{2}{12}$ _____ $\dfrac{1}{6}$

6. $\dfrac{2}{5}$ _____ $\dfrac{4}{6}$

7. $\dfrac{9}{12}$ _____ $\dfrac{7}{4}$

8. $\dfrac{0}{3}$ _____ $\dfrac{0}{8}$

A 12-Cube Box Pattern

The dark squares make the bottom of a rectangular
box that contains exactly 12 cubes. The box has
no top. Draw the sides to finish the pattern for
the box. (Challenge: Can you find all the patterns
that would make a box that holds 12 cubes?)

NOTE Students have
been designing patterns
for boxes (with no tops).

 125–126

© Pearson Education 4

Moving Between Solids and Silhouettes

Finding Volume of More Boxes

How many cubes fit in each box? First, determine the answer without building the box. Then build a box and use cubes to check. For Boxes 2 and 3, also draw the pattern.

	Pattern	**Picture**	**First Answer**	**Actual Answer**
Box 1	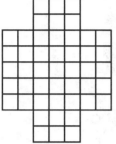		_____	_____
Box 2		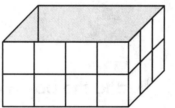	_____	_____
Box 3	The bottom of the box is 4 units by 5 units. The box is 3 units high.		_____	_____

More Building Up

Use graph paper to build a pattern for the boxes described below. You may need more than one sheet of graph paper to complete the pattern.

1. The bottom of the box is 4×3, and the box will hold 36 cubes.

2. The bottom of the box is 3×3, and the box will hold 45 cubes.

3. The bottom of the box is 6×4, and the box will hold 48 cubes.

Challenge: For each problem, can you find other boxes that will hold the same number of cubes?

Double the Number of Cubes

1. You have a box that is 2 by 3 by 4. How many cubes does it hold? How do you know?

2. The factory wants you to build a box that will hold twice as many cubes. Find the dimensions of a box that contains two times as many cubes as a box that is 2 by 3 by 4. Use the space below to draw the box.

3. How many cubes will this new box contain? How do you know?

4. Is the box you found the only box that works? How do you know?

Challenge: See how many boxes you can find that will hold two times as many cubes as a 2 by 3 by 4 box. Show them on a separate sheet of paper.

A Method for Finding Volume

1. Describe a way to determine how many cubes will fit in a rectangular box. Your method should work for any box, whether you start with a box pattern, a picture of the box, or a description of the box in words.

2. Find the number of cubes that fit in a box that is 20 units by 10 units on the bottom and 12 units high. How can you convince your classmates that your answer is correct?

Daily Practice

Portion Puzzles

Solve each problem.

> **NOTE** Students find the total amount given the number of fractional parts.
>
> **SMH** 62

1. How many pies are needed for 12 people to each have $\frac{1}{6}$ of a pie?

2. How many pizzas are needed for 24 people to each have $\frac{1}{4}$ of a pizza?

3. How many sheets of paper are needed for 4 people to each have $3\frac{1}{4}$ sheets?

Finding the Number of Cubes

NOTE Students have been designing patterns for boxes and finding the volume of these boxes. Allow them to use their own strategies for finding the volume of this box.

SMH 125–126

1. How many unit cubes are in this package?

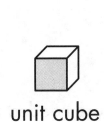

unit cube

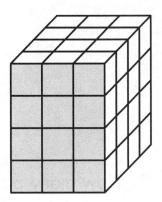

Use the grid on the next page to draw a pattern for this package. Your pattern for the box should completely cover all but the top of the package. The package should completely fill the box.

2. Now how many cubes do you think are in the package?

Daily Practice

All Kinds of Boxes

These patterns make open boxes:

NOTE Students determine the volume of boxes from 2-dimensional patterns.

SMH 125–126

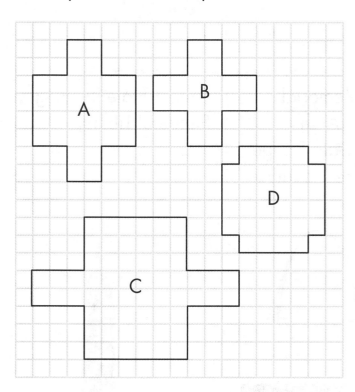

1. Which holds the greatest number of cubes? _____

2. Which box is tallest? _____ Which box is shortest? _____

Ongoing Review

3. How many cubes like the one shown would fit in a box with this pattern?

 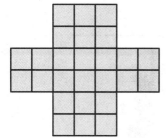

A. 26   **B.** 14   **C.** 12   **D.** 6

American Landmarks

Identify the silhouettes of the American symbols and landmarks listed below.

NOTE Students solve real-world problems involving the math content of this unit.

 122–123

White House	Lincoln Memorial	Empire State Building
Liberty Bell	Gateway Arch	Statue of Liberty
The Alamo	Golden Gate Bridge	
Mississippi Riverboat	The Space Needle	

a.
_____

b.
_____

c.
_____

d.
_____

e.
_____

f.
_____

g.
_____

h.
_____

i.
_____

j.
_____

Polished Spiral Karin Kuhlmann

"Although the creation of fractals is bounded to strict mathematical rules, the results are always very inspiring." – **Karin Kuhlmann**

Student Activity Book

How Many Packages? How Many Groups?   UNIT 8

Investigations
IN NUMBER, DATA, AND SPACE®

How Many Packages?
How Many Groups?

Closest Estimate

Each problem below has a choice of three estimates.
Which one do you think is closest? Circle the closest
estimate. Then write about why you think this estimate is
the closest.

1. The closest estimate for 78 × 7 is: 200   500   700

I think this is closest because:

2. The closest estimate for 18 × 26 is: 400   600   1,000

I think this is closest because:

3. The closest estimate for 32 × 54 is: 500   1,000   1,500

I think this is closest because:

4. Choose one or more of the problems above and solve
it to get an exact answer. Show your solution with
equations. Did you choose the closest estimate?

Stamp Collections

NOTE Students practice solving addition and subtraction problems in a story problem context.

SMH 8–9, 13–15

1. Helena has a collection of stamps. She has 734 South American stamps and 555 African stamps.

   a. How many stamps does Helena have?

   b. How many more stamps does she need to have a total of 1,500 stamps?

2. Terrell also has a stamp collection. He has 839 stamps from Africa and 472 stamps from North America.

   a. How many stamps does Terrell have?

   b. How many more stamps does he need to have a total of 1,500 stamps?

3. How many more stamps does Terrell have in his collection than Helena has in her collection?

More or Less?

Without actually solving each problem, decide whether the answer to each problem is more or less than each of the landmark numbers below the problem. Answer "yes" or "no" on the line next to each question.

NOTE Students practice estimation strategies that include rounding to landmark numbers and using what they know about multiplication facts and multiplying by a multiple of 10.

1. 28×4

   More than 100? _____

   More than 200? _____

2. 30×13

   More than 300? _____

   More than 600? _____

3. 26×43

   More than 500? _____

   More than 1,000? _____

   Less than 1,500? _____

4. Choose one of the problems above and make a close estimate. Write about how you made your estimate, including what numbers you used to help you estimate.

How Many Packages? How Many Groups?

Solving 2-Digit Multiplication Problems (page 1 of 2)

First, write a story to go with each problem. Then, solve the problem and show your solution. You may use arrays or pictures if they help show your strategy more clearly.

1. 53 × 24 = _____

   Story problem:

   Solution:

Solving 2-Digit Multiplication Problems (page 2 of 2)

2. $46 \times 37 = $ _____

Story problem:

Solution:

Multiplying Two Ways

NOTE Students solve the same 2-digit multiplication problem in two different ways.

SMH 40–41, 42

1. Solve this problem in two different ways. Be sure to show how you got your answer.

$31 \times 27 =$ _____

First way:

Second way:

Ongoing Review

2. What is the closest estimate of 39×22?

   A. 400   **B.** 600   **C.** 800   **D.** 1,000

Solving a Multiplication Problem

First, write a story problem for 22×34. Then, solve the problem and show how you solved it. You may include arrays or pictures of groups.

NOTE Students use multiplication strategies that include breaking a problem apart to make smaller problems that are easier to multiply.

SMH 40–41, 42

$22 \times 34 =$ _____

Story problem:

Here's how I solved it:

Two Cluster Problems

Solve the first three problems in each cluster. Show your strategy for solving the final problem. Put a star next to any of the problems in the cluster that helped you.

Set A

Solve these problems:

$4 \times 3 =$

$50 \times 3 =$

$54 \times 10 =$

Now solve $54 \times 13 =$

Set B

Solve these problems:

$2 \times 38 =$

$4 \times 38 =$

$40 \times 38 =$

Now solve $42 \times 38 =$

Adding Two Ways

NOTE Students use different strategies to solve addition problems. They work on efficiency and flexibility by solving the same problem in two different ways.

SMH 8-9

1. Solve this problem in two different ways. Be sure to show how you got your answer.

1,018 + 879 = _____

First way:

Second way:

Ongoing Review

2. 566 + 200 − 20 = _____

A. 786   **B.** 766   **C.** 746   **D.** 546

How Many Packages? How Many Groups?

Multiplication Cluster Problems (page 1 of 2)

In Sets A–F, solve the first three problems in each cluster.
Show your strategy for solving the final problem. Put a star
next to any of the problems in the cluster that helped you.

Set A

Solve these problems:

$6 \times 30 =$

$3 \times 30 =$

$30 \times 30 =$

Now solve $36 \times 33 =$

Set B

Solve these problems:

$7 \times 25 =$

$20 \times 25 =$

$40 \times 25 =$

Now solve $47 \times 25 =$

Set C

Solve these problems:

$3 \times 5 =$

$3 \times 60 =$

$40 \times 60 =$

Now solve $43 \times 65 =$

Multiplication Cluster Problems (page 2 of 2)

Set D

Solve these problems:

$2 \times 57 =$

$4 \times 57 =$

$40 \times 57 =$

Now solve $44 \times 57 =$

Set E

Solve these problems:

$6 \times 25 =$

$60 \times 6 =$

$60 \times 20 =$

Now solve $64 \times 26 =$

Set F

Solve these problems:

$10 \times 45 =$

$9 \times 45 =$

$4 \times 45 =$

Now solve $94 \times 45 =$

Showing Solutions with Arrays

Choose one of the problems from the two previous pages, and write it on this sheet. In the space below, draw an array to show how you can break the problem into easier problems to solve it. Remember to label the dimensions of the array and the products in each part of the array.

Problem: _____

1. Here is one way to show the solution with an array:

CHALLENGE: Show a second way.

Pencil Problems (page 1 of 2)

Read each of the story problems below, and answer each part of the problem. Show your solutions.

1. Lakeside School has 500 students. The principal orders 22 boxes of pencils. Each box has 24 pencils. Will he have enough pencils to give one to each student in the school? Write an estimate and explain your thinking.

   a. How many pencils are there in 22 boxes? Show your solution.

   b. How many more or less than 500 is that?

Pencil Problems (page 2 of 2)

2. The Park City Children's Museum needs 1,000 pencils
for its store. The museum orders pencils in boxes of 48.
Will there be enough pencils if the museum orders
25 boxes? Write an estimate and explain your thinking.

a. How many pencils are there in 25 boxes?
Show your solution.

b. How many more or less than 1,000 is that?

Subtracting Two Ways

1. Solve this problem in two different ways.
   Be sure to show how you got your answer.

NOTE Students use strategies to solve subtraction problems. They work on efficiency and flexibility by solving the same problem in two different ways.

SMH **13–15**

   $30.50 − $17.79 = _____

   First way:

   Second way:

Ongoing Review

2. 32 × 6 = _____

   A. 182   **B.** 186   **C.** 192   **D.** 300

Multiplication Story Problem

NOTE Students make an estimate and solve a multiplication story problem.

SMH **40–41, 42**

1. The school cafeteria serves 700 students during lunch. The disposable trays come in boxes of 36. Will there be enough trays if there are 21 boxes? Write an estimate and explain your thinking.

   a. How many trays are in 21 boxes?
      Show your solution.

   b. How many more or less than 700 is that?

Ongoing Review

2. Which number is **not** a factor of 810?

   A. 405   **B.** 27   **C.** 25   **D.** 3

Problems About Oranges

Solve each story problem. Show your solution.
You may include arrays or pictures of groups.

NOTE Students practice multiplying 2-digit numbers by 2-digit numbers.

SMH **40–41, 42**

1. The Sunshine Fruit Company sells oranges in boxes that hold 72 oranges. Sally Green ordered 35 boxes for her grocery store. How many oranges does Ms. Green have to sell?

2. A fruit stand worker sells bags of oranges. There are 18 oranges in a bag. Over the weekend, the fruit stand worker sold 74 bags. How many oranges did he sell?

© Pearson Education 4

Making an Easier Problem

1. Solve these two problems and show your strategy.

   a. $15 \times 29 =$ **b.** $38 \times 16 =$

2. Read the story below and compare it to the problems above. How would you finish Sophia's and George's strategies?

   The fourth grade is selling oranges to raise money for charity. The oranges come in two sizes of boxes. The large boxes contain 29 oranges each. The small boxes contain 16 oranges each.

   a. Sophia counts up how many large boxes the class sold and counts 15 boxes. To find out how many oranges there are in total in the large boxes, Sophia first multiplies 15 and 30.

   What does Sophia have to do to finish the problem?

   b. George counts up how many small boxes the class sold and counts 38 boxes. Like Sophia, he starts with an easier problem, multiplying 40 and 16.

   What does George have to do to find how many oranges there are in total in the 38 small boxes?

Related Problems

Solve each set of problems below. Show your strategy for the last problem in each set.

1. $7 \times 30 =$

$7 \times 29 =$

This is how I solved 7×29:

2. $20 \times 25 =$

$18 \times 25 =$

This is how I solved 18×25:

3. $3 \times 50 =$

$30 \times 50 =$

$30 \times 49 =$

This is how I solved 30×49:

4. $6 \times 22 =$

$60 \times 22 =$

$59 \times 22 =$

This is how I solved 59×22:

Coin Jars

1. Damian has a coin jar full of pennies, dimes, nickels, and quarters. Most of the coins in his jar are pennies. He knows that there is $7.00 in his coin jar. What combination of coins could be in Damian's coin jar that would equal $7.00?

   First solution: Second solution:

2. Ursula also has a coin jar. There are only two kinds of coins in her coin jar. She knows that there is $3.75 in her jar. What combination of coins could be in Ursula's coin jar that would equal $3.75?

   First solution: Second solution:

Ongoing Review

3. $700 \times 6 =$ _____

   A. 42   **B.** 420   **C.** 4,200   **D.** 42,000

More Related Problems

Solve each pair of problems below. Show your strategy for the second problem in each problem.

NOTE Students practice solving problems in which one factor is 1 or 2 away from a multiple of 10. Sometimes it is helpful to solve problems like these by changing that factor to a nearby multiple of 10 and adjusting the answer.

SMH 40–43

1. $14 \times 20 =$ This is how I solved
$14 \times 19 =$ 14×19:

2. $30 \times 25 =$ This is how I solved 28×25:
$28 \times 25 =$

3. $35 \times 30 =$ This is how I solved 35×29:
$35 \times 29 =$

4. $50 \times 40 =$ This is how I solved 50×38:
$50 \times 38 =$

More Multiplication
Cluster Problems (page 1 of 2)

In Sets A–D, solve each set of problems. Show your
strategy for the problem in the second column.

Set A

Solve these problems:

$30 \times 50 =$

$7 \times 50 =$

$37 \times 2 =$

$3 \times 52 =$

$30 \times 52 =$

Now solve $37 \times 52 =$

Set B

Solve these problems:

$6 \times 6 =$

$60 \times 60 =$

$60 \times 63 =$

$63 \times 60 =$

$3 \times 63 =$

Now solve $63 \times 63 =$

More Multiplication
Cluster Problems (page 2 of 2)

Set C

Solve these problems:

$50 \times 90 =$

$60 \times 90 =$

$9 \times 90 =$

$59 \times 90 =$

$59 \times 3 =$

Now solve $59 \times 93 =$

Set D

Solve these problems:

$8 \times 25 =$

$8 \times 26 =$

$80 \times 26 =$

$85 \times 10 =$

$85 \times 20 =$

Now solve $85 \times 26 =$

Making Cluster Problems (page 1 of 2)

Estimate the answer to each problem. Make up a cluster
of problems to help you solve each problem. Exchange
clusters with a partner and solve each other's clusters.

1. $39 \times 75 =$ Estimate: _____

2. $44 \times 28 =$ Estimate: _____

Making Cluster Problems (page 2 of 2)

3. 64 × 73 =   Estimate: _____

4. 58 × 46 =   Estimate: _____

More Problems About Oranges

Solve each story problem below. Show your solutions.
You may also show your solutions with arrays or pictures
of groups.

1. Annie has filled her delivery truck with 70 boxes of
    oranges. Each box contains 50 oranges. When she gets
    to the supermarket, the grocer wants only 68 boxes. She
    decides to take the extra boxes to the food bank.

    a. How many oranges does Annie have on the truck?

    b. How many oranges does the grocer want?

    c. How many oranges will Annie give the food bank?

2. Jim is packing oranges into boxes that are meant to
    hold 50 oranges. But the oranges are too big! He can
    only fit 49 oranges into each box. He has 36 boxes to
    fill. How many oranges will he need?

Name   Date

Daily Practice

Addition and Subtraction

Solve the problems below. Show your solutions, using clear and concise notation.

NOTE Students practice solving addition and subtraction problems.

SMH 8–9, 13–15

1. 536
      + 647

2. 724
      − 248

3. 851 + 463 = _____

4. 1,250
       − 629

5. _____ + 842 = 1,600

6. 1,200 − _____ = 350

7. _____ + 712 = 1,350

8. 800 − _____ = 499

Solving Another Multiplication Problem

NOTE Students solve a 2-digit multiplication problem.

SMH **40–43**

Write a story problem for 65×35. Then solve the problem and show how you solved it.

1. $65 \times 35 =$ _____

   Story problem:

   Here is how I solved it:

Ongoing Review

2. Which number is **not** a factor of 750?

   A. 250   **B.** 75   **C.** 15   **D.** 7

Division Practice

Solve each division problem below. Then write the
related multiplication combination.

NOTE Students review
division problems that
are related to known
multiplication combinations.

 35

Division Problem	Multiplication Combination
1. 63 ÷ 7 = _____	_____ × _____ = _____
2. 72 ÷ 9 = _____	_____ × _____ = _____
3. 56 ÷ 8 = _____	_____ × _____ = _____
4. 64 ÷ 8 = _____	_____ × _____ = _____
5. 121 ÷ 11 = _____	_____ × _____ = _____
6. 84 ÷ 7 = _____	_____ × _____ = _____
7. 48 ÷ 6 = _____	_____ × _____ = _____
8. 36 ÷ 4 = _____	_____ × _____ = _____
9. $6\overline{)42}$	_____ × _____ = _____
10. $9\overline{)54}$	_____ × _____ = _____

How Many Packages? How Many Groups?

Writing Multiplication Story Problems (page 1 of 2)

Write a story problem for each problem. Then solve the problem and show your solution.

1. 28 × 53 = _____

   Story problem:

   Solution:

2. 83 × 19 = _____

   Story problem:

   Solution:

Writing Multiplication Story Problems (page 2 of 2)

3. $55 \times 74 =$ _____
   Story problem:

   Solution:

4. $67 \times 46 =$ _____
   Story problem:

   Solution:

"How Far?" Problems

Solve the following problems and explain how you found the distance between the numbers.

NOTE Students use addition and subtraction to solve problems.

SMH 13–15

1. How far is it from 752 to 1,000?

2. How far is it from 619 to 2,000?

3. How far is it from 1,345 to 3,000?

4. How far is it from 4,658 to 5,000?

Ongoing Review

5. 8 is a factor of which number?

   A. 50   **B.** 300   **C.** 400   **D.** 500

Name _____ Date _____

How Many Packages? How Many Groups? **Daily Practice**

Selling Fruit

NOTE Students practice solving addition and subtraction problems in a story problem context.

SMH **8–9, 13–15**

1. On Monday, a grocery store received a shipment of 1,000 apples. The apples were quite tasty, and the store sold 346 of them that day. How many apples were left to sell the next day?

2. On Wednesday, the store received a shipment of 1,200 oranges. The store sold 263 oranges that day. How many oranges were left to sell the next day?

3. On Saturday, the store received a shipment of 2,000 mangos. The store sold 415 mangos on Saturday and 680 mangos on Sunday.

   a. How many mangos did the store sell on the weekend (Saturday and Sunday)?

   b. How many mangos were left to sell on Monday morning?

Solving Division Problems

Solve the story problems below. Write an equation for each problem and show how you solved it so that someone else reading this will understand your thinking.

NOTE Students review the meaning of division problems and practice solving them.

 44, 50–52

1. Marco wants to sell his marble collection at a yard sale. He has 112 marbles that he wants to put in bags with 8 marbles in each bag. How many bags of marbles will he have?

   Equation:

   Solution:

2. Marco baked 96 cookies to sell at the yard sale. He wants to fill 6 cookie tins with the same number of cookies in each tin. How many cookies should he put in each tin?

   Equation:

   Solution:

Problems About Teams (page 1 of 2)

Solve each of the story problems and show your solutions. You may also use a picture to explain your thinking.

1. It is field day at Riverside School. All of the fourth graders are outside playing games. There are 126 students. Each team has 14 students. How many teams can they make?

2. There are 112 students in third grade. How many teams of 7 can they make?

3. There are 120 students in fifth grade. How many teams of 15 can they make?

Problems About Teams (page 2 of 2)

4. There are 95 students in second grade. How many teams of 5 can they make?

5. There are 154 students in sixth grade. How many teams of 11 can they make?

6. There are 132 students in first grade. How many teams of 6 can they make?

How Many Hundreds? How Many Total?

NOTE Students estimate and solve addition problems.

SMH 8–9

1. Here are the numbers of postcards in six collections.

   74, 46, 98, 22, 113, 51

   a. About how many hundreds of postcards are there in all?

   Estimate: 300 or 400 or 500 or 600?
   How did you decide?

   b. Add the numbers to find the exact total number of postcards.

2. Here are the costs of 4 items at the grocery store.
   $1.31, $2.71, $1.97, $3.04

   a. About how much do the 4 items cost?
   Estimate: $7.00 or $8.00 or $9.00 or $10.00?
   How did you decide?

   b. Add the numbers to find the exact cost of the 4 items.

Ongoing Review

3. What is 300 more than 2,816?

   A. 5,816   **B.** 3,116   **C.** 2,516   **D.** 2,116

Multiplication Practice

Solve each problem in two ways. Record your solutions.

NOTE Students practice solving 2-digit multiplication problems. They have been working on breaking numbers apart in a variety of ways in order to solve these problems.

 40–43

1. $63 \times 45 =$ _____

   First way:

   Second way:

2. $72 \times 56 =$ _____

   First way:

   Second way:

Marvin's Mystery Multiple Tower

This is the top part of Marvin's multiple tower:

240
224
208
192
176

1. By what number is Marvin counting?

2. How many numbers are in Marvin's tower so far? How do you know?

3. What is Marvin's 10th multiple?

4. If Marvin adds 5 more numbers to his tower, on what number will he land?

Problems About Multiple Towers (page 1 of 2)

1. This is the top part of Malia's multiple tower.

299
276
253
230
207

a. By what number is Malia counting?

b. What is Malia's 10th multiple? How do you know?

c. What is her 20th multiple? How do you know?

2. This is the top part of Marco's multiple tower.

198
180
162
144
126

a. By what number is Marco counting?

b. What is Marco's 5th multiple? How do you know?

c. What will his 15th multiple be? How do you know?

Problems About Multiple Towers (page 2 of 2)

3. This is the top part of Megan's multiple tower.

360
345
330
315
300

a. By what number is Megan counting?

b. How many numbers are in Megan's tower? How do you know?

c. What is her 10th multiple? How do you know?

4. This is the top part of Michael's multiple tower.

651
620
589
558
527

a. By what number is Michael counting?

b. How many numbers are in Michael's tower? How do you know?

c. What will his 25th multiple be? How do you know?

Solving Division Problems (page 1 of 2)

Solve each problem. You may want to represent the
problem with pictures. Show your solutions.

1. You have 3 decks of cards with 52 cards in each deck.
   How many cards will each person get if the 3 decks
   are dealt out evenly to 6 people?

2. Cans of juice come in cases of 24. How many cases
   do you need to give one can to each of 264 students?

3. A lunar month (from the day of the new moon to the
   day of the next new moon) is about 28 days. About
   how many lunar months are in a year (365 days)?

Solving Division Problems (page 2 of 2)

4. $16\overline{)256}$

5. $508 \div 22 =$ _____

6. $360 \div 11 =$ _____

Reading a Long Book

NOTE Students practice solving addition and subtraction problems in a story problem context.

SMH 8, 9, 13–15

1. Noemi borrowed a new book from the library. At 1,000 pages, it is the longest book she has ever tried to read! Today, she read 115 pages. How many more pages does she have to read to reach the end?

2. In the next week, Noemi reads 388 more pages. How many pages has she read in all?

3. At the end of 2 weeks, Noemi has read 816 pages. How many pages does she have left to finish the book?

Ongoing Review

4. How many 1,000s are in 7,010?

   A. 7   **B.** 70   **C.** 700   **D.** 7,000

Solving a Division Story Problem

NOTE Students solve a division problem in a story context.

SMH **46, 52**

1. Ms. Kim's class has 185 books in their classroom library. She puts 45 books on each shelf.

   a. How many shelves have 45 books?

   b. How many books are on the last shelf?

Ongoing Review

2. What is the next multiple in this multiple tower?

   A. 180   **B.** 189   **C.** 191   **D.** 193

162
135
108
81

Writing a Division Story Problem ✎ WRITING

NOTE Students have been working on solving division problems with 2-digit and 3-digit numbers. It is often helpful to think of a division problem in a story context.

SMH 46, 50, 51, 52

1. Choose one of the division problems below and circle it. Write a story problem to go with it. Then solve the division problem, and show your solution. (You may do more than one problem if you have time.)

$$96 \div 12 = \qquad 135 \div 9 = \qquad 169 \div 13 =$$

Story problem:

Solution:

Ongoing Review

2. Richard had $6.47. He spent $4.28 on a poster. How much money does Richard have left?

   A. $10.75   **B.** $2.29   **C.** $2.19   **D.** $1.19

Jill's Multiple Tower

This is the top part of Jill's multiple tower.

NOTE Students solve problems involving multiples.

 SMH **36**

432
405
378
351
324

1. By what number is Jill counting?

2. How many numbers are in Jill's tower so far? How do you know?

3. What is Jill's 10th multiple?

4. Imagine that Jill adds more multiples to her tower. What would be the 20th multiple in her tower? How do you know?

Ongoing Review

5. What is the closest estimate of 375 ÷ 23?

A. 10   **B.** 15   **C.** 30   **D.** 150

Division Problems About Pencils

NOTE Students practice understanding story problems and solving division problems.

SMH 48–49, 50–52

Solve each problem below and show your solutions. You need these two pieces of information for these problems.

- Pencils come in packages of 12.
- There are 23 students in Mr. Coburn's class.

1. How many packages of pencils does Mr. Coburn have to open to give 2 pencils to everyone in his class?

2. How many packages of pencils does Mr. Coburn have to open to give 4 pencils to everyone in his class?

3. How many packages of pencils does Mr. Coburn have to open to give 6 pencils to everyone in his class?

Solving Multiplication and Division Problems (page 1 of 2)

For each problem below, first make a close estimate. Then solve each problem, and show your work.

1. Cory buys stickers in packages of 36 for his sticker collection. Last year, he bought 97 packages of stickers. How many stickers did he buy?

   Estimate:

   Solution:

2. Tanya has 460 sports cards in her collection, which she keeps in a binder that holds 8 cards on a page. How many pages has she filled?

   Estimate:

   Solution:

Solving Multiplication and Division Problems (page 2 of 2)

3. The city soccer league has 273 players who have signed up to play on teams. They want to make 18 teams. How many players can they put on each team?

Estimate:

Solution:

4. The fourth graders sold packages of seeds to raise money for their class trip. Each package costs $0.75. The students sold 62 packages in all. How much money did they raise?

Estimate:

Solution:

School Supplies

NOTE Students practice solving addition and subtraction problems in a story problem context.

SMH 8–9, 13–15

1. Mr. Mancillas had $200 to spend on art supplies. He spent $103.80 on drawing paper and $86.35 on paintbrushes.

   a. How much did he spend on art supplies?

   b. How much money did he have left after he bought the supplies?

2. Ms. Kim had $300 to spend on science supplies. She spent $77.49 on thermometers and $212.99 on a microscope.

   a. How much did she spend on science materials?

   b. How much money did she have left after she bought science materials?

Ongoing Review

3. Which of the following is true?

   A. $875 - 476 > 400$ **C.** $640 - 139 < 500$

   B. $933 - 734 < 200$ **D.** $521 - 420 < 100$

Say Cheese! (page 1 of 2)

Use the data below to solve Problems 1–3.
Show your work on another sheet of paper.

NOTE Students solve real-world problems involving the math content of this unit.

SMH 40–43, 50–52

Film	Number of pictures
PF-12	12
PF-24	24
PF-36	36

1. Mandy bought 15 rolls of PF-12 film for summer camp.
   How many pictures can she take?

2. Paco took 288 pictures, using rolls of PF-36 film.
   How many rolls did he use?

Say Cheese! (page 2 of 2)

3. Monroe School has 753 students. The Family Club is taking a picture of every student in the school. How many rolls of PF-24 will the club need to buy?

4. Sylvia has a digital camera. Instead of film, her camera uses a memory card that stores 26 pictures. When the card is filled, she transfers the pictures to her computer and uses the card again. Last summer, she took 416 pictures. How many times did Sylvia fill the memory card?

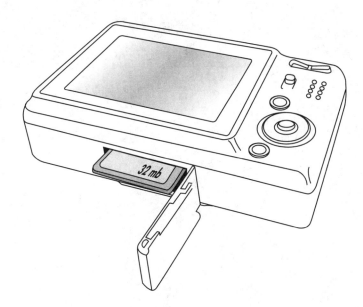

Polished Spiral Karin Kuhlmann

"Although the creation of fractals is bounded to strict mathematical rules, the results are always very inspiring."– **Karin Kuhlmann**

Investigations
IN NUMBER, DATA, AND SPACE®

Penny Jars and Plant Growth

Investigation 3

Penny Jars and Plant Growth

Plant Height Chart (page 1 of 2)

Plant Name _____

Date	Day of the Week	Height	Comments

Penny Jars and Plant Growth

Plant Height Chart (page 2 of 2)

Date	Day of the Week	Height	Comments

Penny Jars and Plant Growth

Temperatures in Two Cities (page 1 of 2)

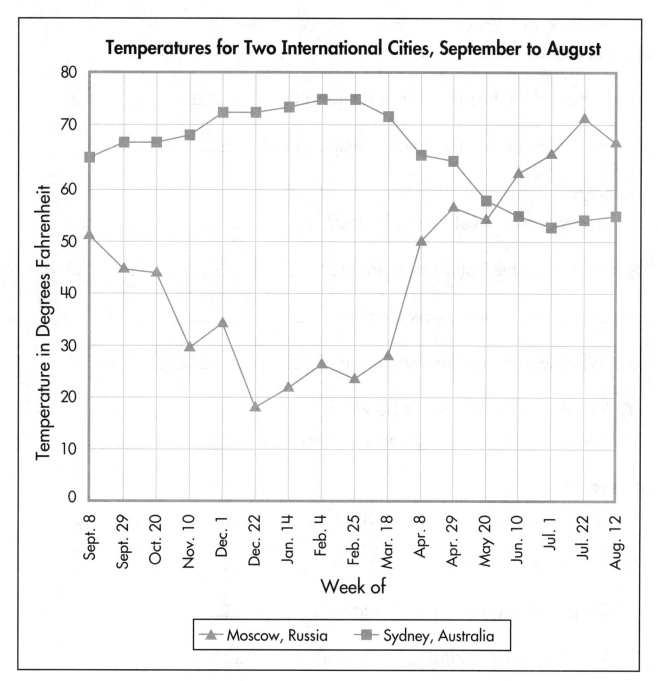

Temperatures for Two International Cities, September to August

Week of

Temperature in Degrees Fahrenheit

▲ Moscow, Russia   ■ Sydney, Australia

Temperatures in Two Cities (page 2 of 2)

Look at the graph on the previous page to answer
these questions:

1. Which place has the hottest temperature? _____

2. Which place has the coldest temperature? _____

Sydney:

3. During which week was it hottest? _____

4. What was the hottest temperature? _____

5. During which week was it coldest? _____

6. What was the coldest temperature? _____

7. What was the difference between
Sydney's hottest and coldest temperatures? _____

Moscow:

8. During which week was it hottest? _____

9. What was the hottest temperature? _____

10. During which week was it coldest? _____

11. What was the coldest temperature? _____

12. What was the difference between
Moscow's hottest and coldest temperatures? _____

Penny Jars and Plant Growth

The Motion Graph (page 1 of 2)

This graph shows a runner's speed during a race.

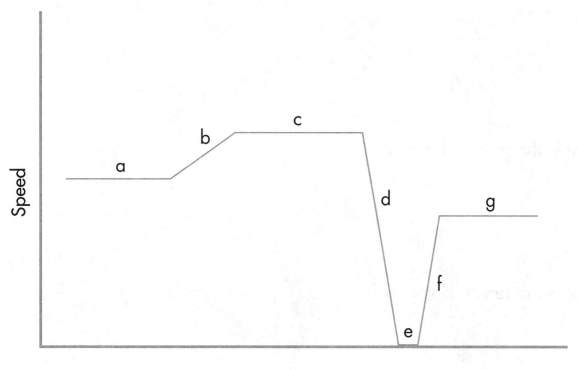

1. At which point is the runner speeding up?

2. At which point has the runner stopped?

The Motion Graph (page 2 of 2)

3. At which point is the runner going at a slow, steady speed?

4. What is the runner doing at d?

5. What is the runner doing at f?

6. What is the runner doing at c?

7. What might have happened to this runner during the race? Tell the whole story on another sheet of paper.

Temperatures for a Day in June: Anchorage, Alaska

NOTE Students plot points on a graph of temperature changes.

SMH 72, 73, 74

1. Here is a table that shows the temperature at different times during a June day in Alaska. (F stands for Fahrenheit.) Make a graph of the data on the grid below.

Time	Temperature
3:00 A.M.	39°F
6:00 A.M.	47°F
9:00 A.M.	52°F
12:00 noon	57°F
3:00 P.M.	60°F
6:00 P.M.	58°F
9:00 P.M.	55°F
12:00 midnight	47°F

2. At what time is it the warmest on this day in June?

   _____

3. At what time is it the coldest?

   _____

Ongoing Review

4. How does the temperature change from noon to midnight?

   A. It gets colder.

   B. It gets warmer.

   C. It gets warmer, and then colder.

   D. It stays the same.

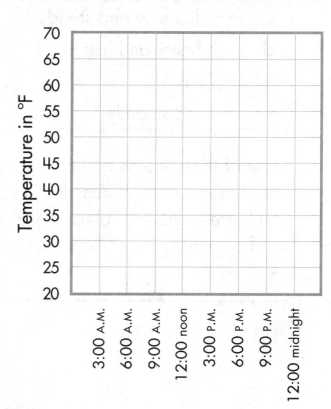

The Boston Marathon (page 1 of 3)

The next pages tell the story of Bobby Hall's experience racing in the Boston Marathon in a wheelchair. The underlined words in the story describe his speed and how it changed throughout the race.

1. Make a graph of the racer's speed over the course of the race.

2. Find the places on your graph where the racer is doing what the underlined words describe. Write the words on your graph in the right place.

   Here is a list of the underlined words in the story.

a. wheeled very fast	**g.** gradually slowing down
b. slowed down a bit	**h.** kept pushing slowly
c. wheeled nice and steady	**i.** picked up the pace
d. push faster and faster	**j.** ran my fastest
e. stopped	**k.** wheeled around slowly
f. wheeled steadily	

3. Some of these words and phrases describe the racer's speed. Some of them describe a **change** in speed. Sort these words and phrases into two lists. Put each word or phrase under the correct heading below.

Speed	Change in Speed

The Boston Marathon (page 2 of 3)

Participating in the Boston Marathon—all 26.2 miles of it—
is an incredible experience. You're with thousands of other
people, going through all kinds of different towns and cities
and college campuses. Wheelchair participants get a lot of
attention in Boston. People know us and they start us right
at the front.

In the beginning of the race, there's about 4 miles of
downhill. Like most wheelchair participants, I <u>wheeled
very fast</u> on that downhill part. It felt good. But at mile 4,
I remembered to pace myself. I <u>slowed down a bit</u>. For
the next 9 miles or so, I <u>wheeled nice and steady</u>.

But then a very exciting thing happened. At Wellesley
College, there was a huge crowd of students lining the
course, screaming and clapping like crazy. All that
excitement made me <u>push faster and faster</u> through the
mile-long part of Wellesley. But then I noticed I was tired—
too tired for being just a little more than halfway through
the race. I <u>stopped</u> for a few seconds to get some water
and pour some over my head. (I was getting hot, too!)
I knew the hardest part of the race was coming up.

After Wellesley, I <u>wheeled steadily</u> for a few more miles.
But then, by the seventeenth mile, it started getting hard.
From mile 17 to 21 or so, I could feel myself <u>gradually
slowing down</u>. There's a bunch of hard hills, and I knew
I just had to take it easy to make it over those hills. My
arms were aching so much. But the funny thing was, even
once I had made it over the hills, I <u>kept pushing slowly</u>.

The Boston Marathon (page 3 of 3)

I think by 21 miles, I was running out of steam. It was hard to keep picking up my arms. Between 21 and 25 miles, I kept pushing slowly.

By 25 miles, I knew I would make it and I picked up the pace. The crowd was tremendous in the last mile or so. They just wouldn't let you slow down. The final stretch of a quarter mile or so is downhill, and I actually wheeled my fastest for that stretch. My arms felt all beaten up and shaky at the finish—but I wheeled around slowly for a while afterwards. That helps you keep from getting so stiff the next day.

—Bobby Hall (from a telephone interview)

Barney's Mystery Multiple Tower

NOTE Students find factors and multiples using a multiple tower.

SMH 36

The picture shows part of Barney's multiple tower.

1. What number is Barney counting by?

2. How many numbers are in Barney's tower so far? How do you know?

3. If Barney adds five more numbers to his tower, what number will he land on?

594
567
540
513
486

Ongoing Review

4. What is Barney's 15th multiple?

A. 15 **B.** 275 **C.** 405 **D.** 450

Name	Date

Penny Jars and Plant Growth

Homework

Temperatures for a Day in June: El Paso, Texas

NOTE Students plot points on a graph of temperature changes.

SMH **72–76**

1. Here is a table that shows the temperature at different times during a June day in Texas. (F stands for Fahrenheit.) Make a graph of the data on the grid below.

Time	Temperature
3:00 A.M.	72°F
6:00 A.M.	70°F
9:00 A.M.	73°F
12:00 noon	80°F
3:00 P.M.	87°F
6:00 P.M.	87°F
9:00 P.M.	84°F
12:00 midnight	80°F

2. At what time is it the warmest on this day in June?

_____

3. At what time is it the coolest?

_____

4. How does the temperature change between 3:00 a.m. and midnight?

_____

_____

_____

_____

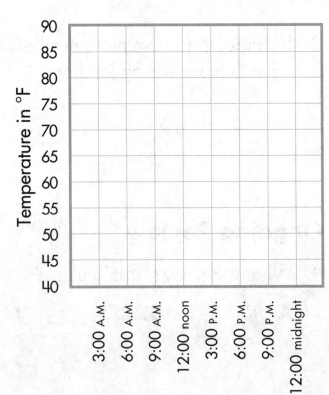

© Pearson Education 4

12 Unit 9

Session 1.2

Penny Jar Amounts

1. Fill in the numbers for your first Penny Jar situation:

   a. Start with _____ pennies. Add _____ pennies each round.

   b. How many pennies are in the jar after 6 rounds?

2. Fill in the numbers for your second Penny Jar situation:

   a. Start with _____ pennies. Add _____ pennies each round.

   b. How many pennies are in the jar after 6 rounds?

A Vegetable Farm

Solve each story problem below and show your solutions. You may also use a picture to explain your thinking.

NOTE Students practice solving multiplication and division problems in story problem contexts.

SMH 45

1. Ms. Mason is packing pumpkins into crates. She has 216 pumpkins, and each crate can hold 8 pumpkins. How many crates does she need?

2. Mr. Lee needs to pack potatoes. He has 24 sacks to pack 288 potatoes. How many potatoes can he put in each sack?

3. Mr. Gorton stores corn in boxes. There are 47 boxes with 95 ears of corn in each box. How much corn does he store?

Penny Jars and Plant Growth   Homework

A Race or Trip

NOTE In this homework, students practice making connections between a story and a graph.

SMH 75–76

1. Write a simple story about a race or trip that involves changing speeds.

2. Now sketch a line graph to show how speed changes in your story.

Penny Jar Table (page 1 of 2)

1. a. Fill in the numbers for a Penny Jar situation:
Start with _____ pennies. Add _____ pennies each round.

b. Complete this table:

Number of Rounds	Total Number of Pennies
Start with	
1	
2	
3	
4	
5	
6	
7	
10	
15	
20	

Penny Jar Table (page 2 of 2)

2. How did you determine the number of pennies for round 10?

3. How did you determine the number of pennies for round 20?

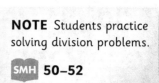

Solving Division Problems

NOTE Students practice
solving division problems.

SMH 50–52

Solve each problem. Show your solutions.

1. 21)‾352‾

2. 459 ÷ 17 = _____

3. Venetta has 405 pictures to put in an album. Each
    page of an album holds 12 pictures. How many pages
    does Venetta need for all of her pictures?

Ongoing Review

4. Which number is **not** a multiple of 24?

    A. 120   **B.** 264   **C.** 300   **D.** 360

Adding Pennies to a Penny Jar 1

> **NOTE** Students have been working with these Penny Jar situations in class. They use what they know about the start amount and the repeated change to figure out the total number of pennies at a future point.
>
> SMH **78, 79**

There are 8 pennies in the jar at the start.
We add 5 pennies each round.

After 1 round there are 13 pennies.

1. How many pennies are in the jar after 2 rounds?

2. How many pennies are in the jar after 4 rounds?

3. How many pennies are in the jar after 6 rounds?
How do you know?

4. Use a picture, diagram, or table to represent this Penny
Jar situation in the space below.

Penny Jars and Plant Growth

Round 20 (page 1 of 2) ✏️ WRITING

Here is a Penny Jar Situation: Start with 5 pennies.
Add 6 pennies each round.

1. Complete this table for this Penny Jar situation.

Number of Rounds	Calculation	Total Number of Pennies
5		
10		
15		
20		

2. How did you find the amount for round 20?

Round 20 (page 2 of 2)

3. Jake says that the total number of pennies for round 20 is double the number for round 10 because the double of 10 is 20. Marisol disagrees and says that Jake's method will not work. Do you agree with Jake or with Marisol? Why?

    a. Write your explanation in words.

    b. Create a representation for this Penny Jar situation that shows your ideas about whether doubling works.

Adding Pennies to a Penny Jar 2

NOTE Students are using a table to record what happens in a situation of constant change. They have been working with these Penny Jar situations in class. They use what they know to figure out the total number of pennies at a future point.

SMH 78, 80

There is 1 penny in the jar at the start.
We add 4 pennies each round.

After 1 round there are 5 pennies.

1. Complete this table to show what happens for 7 rounds.

Number of Rounds	Total Number of Pennies
Start with	
1	
2	
3	
4	
5	
6	
7	

2. How many pennies will there be in the jar after 10 rounds? How did you figure this out?

Solve in Two Ways, Multiplication

NOTE Students practice solving 2-digit multiplication problems. They work on efficiency and flexibility by solving the problem in two ways.

SMH 40–43

Solve each problem in two ways.
Record your solutions.

1. $76 \times 29 =$ _____

    First way:

    Second way:

2. $34 \times 88 =$ _____

    First way:

    Second way:

Matching Tables and Graphs (page 1 of 2)

Which table goes with Graph 1? How do you know?

Graph 1

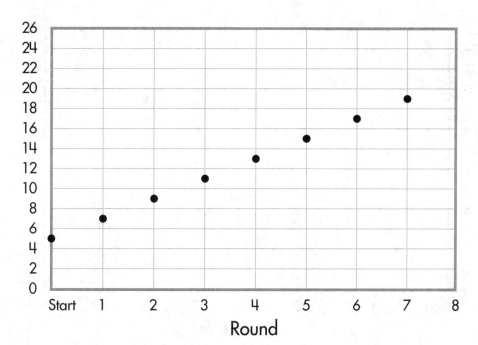

Tape or glue
the matching
table here.

Matching Tables and Graphs (page 2 of 2)

Which table goes with Graph 2? How do you know?

Graph 2

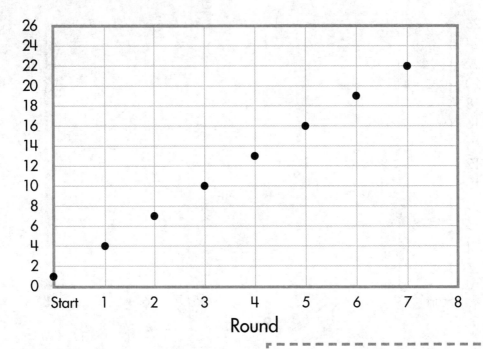

Tape or glue
the matching
table here.

Penny Jars and Plant Growth

Graphing a Penny Jar (page 1 of 2)

Start with _____ pennies. Add _____ pennies each round.

1. Complete this table:

Number of Rounds	Total Number of Pennies
Start with	
1	
2	
3	
4	
5	
6	
7	
10	
15	
20	

2. How many pennies are there after 30 rounds? _____

3. How many pennies are there after 50 rounds? _____

4. How many pennies are there after 100 rounds? _____

5. How did you figure out the number of pennies after 100 rounds? Use number sentences to show what you did.

_____

Graphing a Penny Jar (page 2 of 2)

6. Make a graph for your Penny Jar situation.

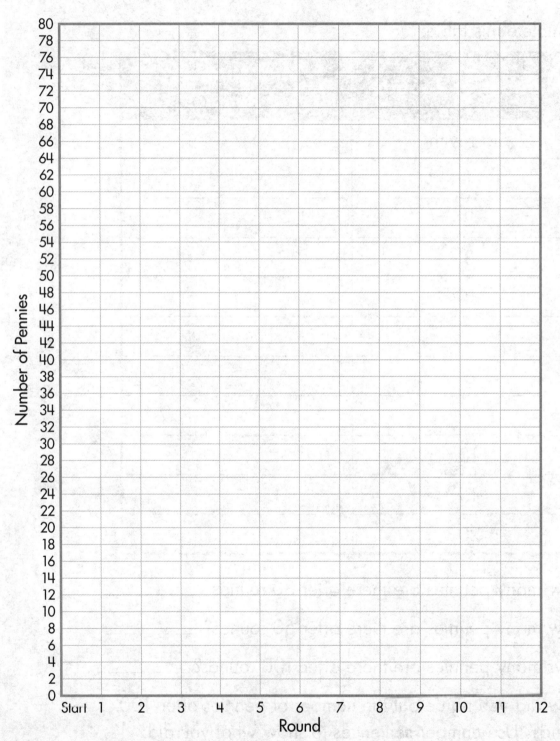

Name _____   Date _____

Daily Practice

How Many Windows?
How Many Cars?

> **NOTE** Students practice solving multiplication and division problems.
>
> SMH 45

Solve each problem below. Show your work.

1. There are 625 windows on Steve's apartment building. Each floor of the building has the same number of windows. If the building is 25 stories tall, how many windows are on each floor?

2. The office building next to Steve's apartment is 77 stories tall. If there are 44 windows on each floor, how many windows are there in all?

Ongoing Review

3. When the parking garage is completely full, it holds 900 cars. There are 12 levels in the garage. Each level holds the same number of cars. How many cars can be parked on each level?

   A. 15   **B.** 20   **C.** 25   **D.** 75

© Pearson Education 4

Penny Jar Tables (page 1 of 2)

Here are the tables for two Penny Jar situations. Complete the tables and then show how you figured out the answers to the questions.

> **NOTE** Students fill in missing values in tables and determine values for later rounds in two Penny Jar situations.
>
> **SMH** 78, 80

Table A

Number of Rounds	Total Number of Pennies
Start with	7
1	11
2	
3	
4	23
5	27
6	
7	

1. How many pennies are there after 10 rounds? _____

2. How many pennies are there after 20 rounds? _____

Penny Jar Tables (page 2 of 2)

Table B

Number of Rounds	Total Number of Pennies
Start with	6
1	
2	16
3	
4	26
5	
6	36
7	

3. How many pennies are there after 10 rounds? _____

4. How many pennies are there after 20 rounds? _____

32 Unit 9

Windows and Towers (page 1 of 2)

1. Fill in the table for the single tower.

Single Tower

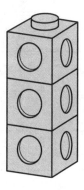

Number of Floors	Number of Windows
1	
2	
3	
4	
5	
6	
7	
8	
9	
10	

2. a. How did you figure out the number of windows on 10 floors?

   b. Write an arithmetic expression that shows how you figured this out.

3. a. How many windows are there on 15 floors?

   b. Write an arithmetic expression that shows how you figured this out.

Windows and Towers (page 2 of 2)

4. Fill in the table for the double tower.

Double Tower

Number of Floors	Number of Windows
1	
2	
3	
4	
5	
6	
7	
8	
9	
10	

5. **a.** How did you figure out the number of windows on 10 floors?

   b. Write an arithmetic expression that shows how you figured this out.

6. **a.** How many windows are there on 15 floors?

   b. Write an arithmetic expression that shows how you figured this out.

Penny Jar Comparisons (page 1 of 3)

1. Card number: _____

2. Situation A: Start with _____ pennies. Add _____ each round.

3. Situation B: Start with _____ pennies. Add _____ each round.

4. Complete the table below:

Round	Situation A: Total Number of Pennies	Situation B: Total Number of Pennies
Starts with		
1		
2		
3		
4		
5		
6		
7		
10		
15		
20		

5. What do you notice about the table? Write your answer on another sheet of paper.

Penny Jar Comparisons (page 2 of 3)

6. Show each Penny Jar situation on the graph.
   Use a different color for each situation.

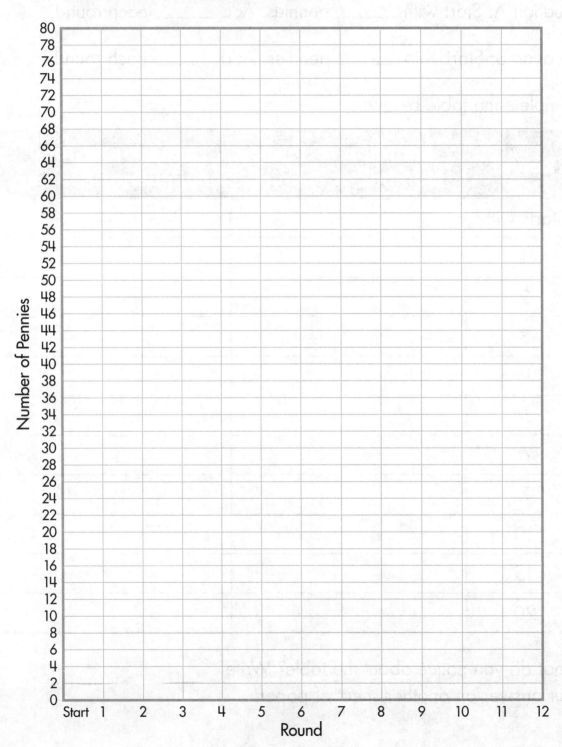

Penny Jar Comparisons (page 3 of 3)

7. What do you notice about the graph?

_____

_____

_____

_____

_____

8. Does Penny Jar B ever have as many pennies
as Penny Jar A? How do you know?

Estimate and Solve

Make an estimate for each problem. Then solve the problem. Show your solution.

NOTE Students first make an estimate and then solve multiplication problems.

SMH **40–43**

1. $53 \times 71 =$

Estimate: _____

Solve:

2. $18 \times 93 =$

Estimate: _____

Solve:

3. $45 \times 55 =$

Estimate: _____

Solve:

Ongoing Review

4. What is the closest estimate for $420 \div 15$?

   A. 20   **B.** 30   **C.** 40   **D.** 42

Your Own Penny Jar

Make up a Penny Jar situation.

NOTE Students complete a table and figure out what will happen later in the sequence.

SMH 78, 80

1. Start with: _____

   Add each round: _____

2. Complete this table:

Number of Rounds	Total Number of Pennies
Start with	
1	
2	
3	
4	
5	
10	
15	
20	

3. Write an arithmetic expression for how many pennies will be in the jar after 100 rounds.

Penny Jars and Plant Growth

Backward Problems for Single and Double Towers (page 1 of 2)

Single Towers

Can a single tower ever have exactly this many windows?
Circle Yes or No. If yes, write how many floors the
tower has.

1. 60 windows?

Yes   No

2. 61 windows?

Yes   No

3. 62 windows?

Yes   No

4. 63 windows?

Yes   No

5. 64 windows?

Yes   No

6. 65 windows?

Yes   No

7. How can you tell whether a single tower can have
exactly 105 windows? And if it does, how can you
figure out the number of floors it has?

Backward Problems for
Single and Double Towers (page 2 of 2)

Double Towers

Can a double tower ever have exactly this many windows?
Circle Yes or No. If yes, write how many floors the
tower has.

8. 80 windows? Yes No	**9.** 81 windows? Yes No
10. 82 windows? Yes No	**11.** 83 windows? Yes No
12. 84 windows? Yes No	**13.** 85 windows? Yes No

14. How can you tell whether a double tower can have
exactly 108 windows? And if it does, how can you
figure out the number of floors it has?

Square and Corner Towers (page 1 of 2)

Fill in the tables and answer the questions.

Square Towers

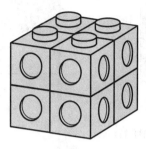

Number of Floors	Number of Windows
1	
2	
3	
4	
5	
6	
7	
8	
9	
10	

1. a. How did you figure out the number of windows on 10 floors?

b. Write an arithmetic expression that shows how you figured this out.

2. a. How many windows are there on 100 floors?

b. Write an arithmetic expression that shows how you figured this out.

Square and Corner Towers (page 2 of 2)

Corner Towers

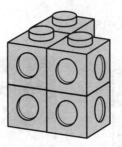

Number of Floors	Number of Windows
1	
2	
3	
4	
5	
6	
7	
8	
9	
10	

3. a. How did you figure out the number of windows on 10 floors?

b. Write an arithmetic expression that shows how you figured this out.

4. a. How many windows are there on 100 floors?

b. Write an arithmetic expression that shows how you figured this out.

Backward Problems for Square and Corner Towers (page 1 of 2)

Square Towers

Can a square tower ever have exactly this many windows?
Circle Yes or No. If yes, write how many floors the
tower has.

1. 90 windows? Yes No	**2.** 91 windows? Yes No
3. 92 windows? Yes No	**4.** 93 windows? Yes No
5. 94 windows? Yes No	**6.** 95 windows? Yes No

7. How can you tell whether a square tower can have
exactly 135 windows? And if it does, how can you
figure out the number of floors it has?

Backward Problems for Square and Corner Towers (page 2 of 2)

Corner Towers

Can a corner tower ever have exactly this many windows?
Circle Yes or No. If yes, write how many floors the
tower has.

8. 90 windows? Yes No	**9.** 91 windows? Yes No
10. 92 windows? Yes No	**11.** 93 windows? Yes No
12. 94 windows? Yes No	**13.** 95 windows? Yes No

14. How can you tell whether a corner tower can have
exactly 123 windows? And if it does, how can you
figure out the number of floors it has?

Daily Practice

The Shape of Graphs

NOTE Students tell the story of a line graph about speed.

 75–76

1. These four graphs each show the speed of a different rider in a long-distance bike ride. Draw a line matching each graph to the description that fits it best.

a. The rider begins the race by speeding up quickly, then slows down and stays at a mostly steady pace for the rest of the race.

b. The rider's pace is fastest during the middle of the race.

c. The rider speeds up and slows down several times during the race.

d. The rider's pace gets steadily faster as the race goes on.

1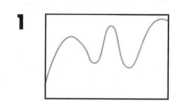

2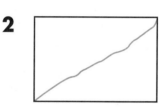

3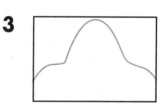

4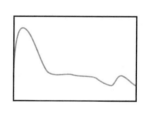

Ongoing Review

2. Which graph shows a rider who ended the race at about the same speed as she began?

A. Graph 3

C. All of the graphs

B. Graphs 3 and 4

D. None of the graphs

Solving Multiplication Problems

NOTE Students practice solving
2-digit multiplication problems.

SMH 40–43

Solve each problem and show your work.

1. $49 \times 25 = $ _____

2. $60 \times 76 = $ _____

3.   32
       $\times$ 43

4.   78
       $\times$ 45

Solve in Two Ways

Solve each problem in two ways.
Show your solution.

NOTE Students solve multiplication and division problems in two ways.

SMH 40–43, 50–52

1. $741 \div 19 =$ _____

First way:

Second way:

2. $66 \times 34 =$ _____

First way:

Second way:

Ongoing Review

3. What is the closest estimate of 38×43?

   A. 120   **B.** 160   **C.** 1,200   **D.** 1,600

A Table, a Graph, and a Rule (page 1 of 2)

Here is a Penny Jar situation: Start with 26 pennies. Add 4 pennies each round.

NOTE Students are working on making and interpreting tables and graphs. They are also making general rules for finding any number of pennies in the Penny Jar.

SMH **78, 80, 81, 86**

1. Make a table to show what happens for 8 rounds. Then graph your data on the following page.

Number of Rounds	Total Number of Pennies
Start with	
1	
2	
3	
4	
5	
6	
7	
8	

2. How many pennies will be in the jar after 30 rounds? Show how you figured this out.

3. Write a rule for the number of pennies for any round. You can use words or an arithmetic expression.

A Table, a Graph, and a Rule (page 2 of 2)

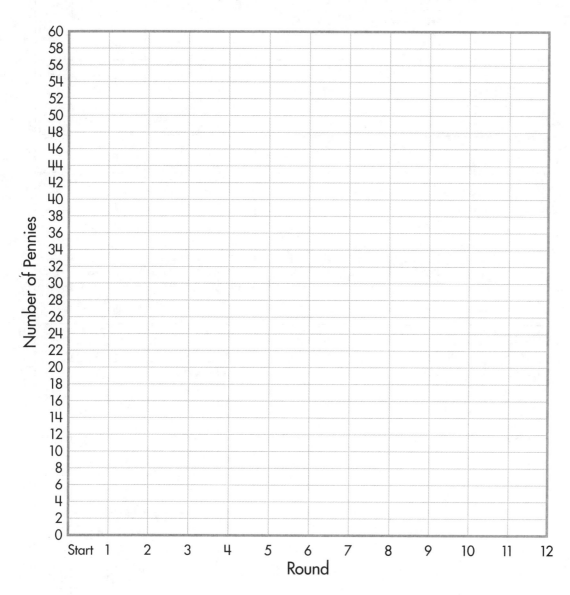

Rules for Towers: Singles and Doubles

1. For a **single** tower, how would you find the number of windows
   a. if there are 20 floors?

   b. if there are 30 floors?

   c. if there are 45 floors?

2. Write a rule for finding the number of windows on a single tower for any number of floors. You can use words or numbers and letters.

3. For a **double** tower, how would you find the number of windows
   a. if there are 20 floors?

   b. if there are 30 floors?

   c. if there are 45 floors?

4. Write a rule for finding the number of windows on a double tower for any number of floors. You can use words or numbers and letters.

Rules for Towers: Corners and Squares

1. For a **corner** tower, how would you find the number of windows

    a. if there are 20 floors?

    b. if there are 30 floors?

    c. if there are 45 floors?

2. Write a rule for finding the number of windows on a corner tower for any number of floors. You can use words or numbers and letters.

3. For a **square** tower, how would you find the number of windows

    a. if there are 20 floors?

    b. if there are 30 floors?

    c. if there are 45 floors?

4. Write a rule for finding the number of windows on a square tower for any number of floors. You can use words or numbers and letters.

Summer Reading

Solve each story problem and show your solutions.

NOTE Students practice solving multiplication and division problems in story problem contexts.

SMH 45

1. Tiana has a new 364-page book to read when she goes on vacation. She is going on vacation for 14 days, and she wants to read the same number of pages each day. How many pages will she read each day?

2. Daniel signed up for a summer reading challenge. He wants to read 75 pages every day in July. There are 31 days in July. How many pages will he read in July?

3. Kate plans to read 35 pages every day in July and 40 pages every day in August. There are 31 days in August, too.

   a. How many pages will Kate read in July?

   b. How many pages will Kate read in August?

Penny Jar Problems (page 1 of 2)

NOTE Students are using tables to help them think about number relationships.

SMH 80

1. Fill out the table for the following Penny Jar situation: Start with 2 pennies. Add 4 pennies each round.

Number of Rounds	Number of Pennies
Start with	
1	
2	
3	
4	
5	

2. Is there ever a round when you will have exactly 50 pennies in the Penny Jar? If so, what round will that be? How do you know?

3. Is there ever a round when you will have exactly 51 pennies in the Penny Jar? If so, what round will that be? How do you know?

Penny Jar Problems (page 2 of 2)

4. Which of these amounts cannot be in the jar: 52, 53, or 54 pennies?

5. Choose one number that will be in the Penny Jar and explain how you know.

6. Choose one number that you know can never be in the Penny Jar and explain how you know.

58 Unit 9

Fast and Slow Growth

1. a. Where does this graph show the **fastest** growth? Circle this on the graph.

b. How can you tell from the **shape** of the graph?

c. How can you tell from the **numbers** along the graph?

Day	Height
Thursday	3 cm
Friday	4 cm
Monday	10 cm
Tuesday	13.5 cm
Wednesday	15 cm
Thursday	16 cm
Friday	16.5 cm
Monday	17 cm

2. a. Where does this graph show the **slowest** growth? Circle this on the graph.

b. How can you tell from the **shape** of the graph?

c. How can you tell from the **numbers** along the graph?

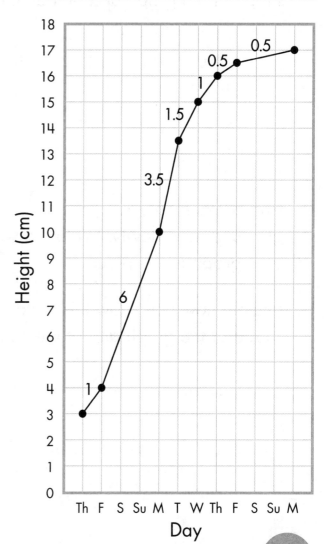

Our Growing Plants

Use this sheet with the graph you have made
of your growing plant.

1. On the graph of your growing plant, write the changes
   (in centimeters) on each section of the line.

2. Find a place on your graph where your plant was
   growing quickly. Write the word "fast" along your
   graph in this place.

3. Explain how you know this is fast growth. Look at the
   shape of the graph and at the numbers on your graph.

4. Find a place on your graph where your plant was
   growing more slowly. Write the word "slow" along
   your graph in this place.

5. Explain how you know this is slow growth. Look at the
   shape of the graph and at the numbers on your graph.

Whose Graph Is It?

NOTE Students tell the story of a line graph about speed.

SMH **75–76**

In the famous race between a tortoise and a hare, the hare sped off and was so confident that he could win the race that he took time for a nap!

Meanwhile, the tortoise kept a slow but steady pace. By the time the hare woke up and started running again, the tortoise was just crossing the finish line.

1. Which graph shows the tortoise's speed?
   Which shows the hare's speed?
   Explain your thinking.

A. 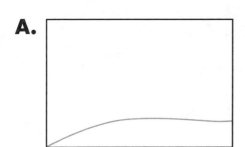   **B.**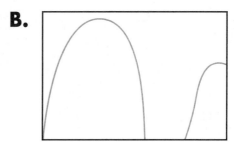

_____

_____

_____

_____

2. Circle True or False about the following statement:
   Even though the tortoise won the race, his ending speed was slower than the hare's ending speed.

   A. True   **B.** False

Writing Multiplication Story Problems

NOTE Students practice solving 2-digit multiplication problems.

SMH 40–43

For each problem, write a story problem. Then solve the problem and show your solution.

1. $82 \times 39 =$ _____
Story problem:

Solution:

2. $56 \times 91 =$ _____
Story problem:

Solution:

A Plant Story

The plant graph shown here has been divided into six parts.

NOTE Students tell the story of a line graph about plant growth.

 SMH 75–77

1. Write a story that makes sense for each part of the plant's growth. Part A has been done for you.

   Part A: The plant started growing slowly.

   Part B: _____

   Part C: _____

   Part D: _____

   Part E: _____

   Part F: _____

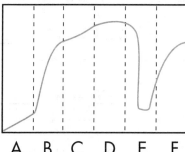

Ongoing Review

2. Which sequence describes the changes shown in the graph?

   A. + + + 0 − − +

   B. − + + + − − +

   C. − + + 0 − − +

   D. 0 + + 0 − − 0

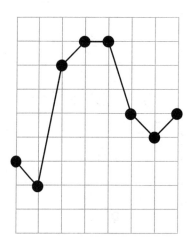

Division Practice

Solve each division problem.
Then write the related
multiplication combination.

NOTE Students are reviewing division problems that are related to the multiplication combinations they know.

SMH 35

Division Problem	Multiplication Combination
1. 144 ÷ 12 = _____	_____ × _____ = _____
2. 32 ÷ 8 = _____	_____ × _____ = _____
3. 28 ÷ 4 = _____	_____ × _____ = _____
4. 56 ÷ 7 = _____	_____ × _____ = _____
5. 110 ÷ 11 = _____	_____ × _____ = _____
6. 64 ÷ 8 = _____	_____ × _____ = _____
7. 63 ÷ 9 = _____	_____ × _____ = _____
8. 27 ÷ 3 = _____	_____ × _____ = _____
9. 7)49	_____ × _____ = _____
10. 9)81	_____ × _____ = _____

Pizza Problems

Solve each story problem and show your
solutions. You may also use a picture to
explain your thinking.

NOTE Students practice solving
multistep story problems involving
multiplication and division.

1. There are 11 people at a pizza party. Each person
   wants 3 slices of pizza, and each pizza has 8 slices.
   How many pizzas should they order?

2. At a larger pizza party, there are 18 people. Each
   person wants 3 slices, and each pizza has 8 slices.
   How many pizzas should they order?

3. At a smaller pizza party, there are 7 people. They order
   3 pizzas. Each person eats 3 slices, and each pizza has
   8 slices. How much extra pizza do they have?

A Penny Jar Story (page 1 of 2)

Here is a Penny Jar situation: Start with
1 penny. Add 3 pennies each round.

NOTE Students make a table
and a graph for a Penny Jar
situation. They also show how
they would figure out what
happens after round 20.

SMH **80–81**

1. Make a table for the first 8 rounds
   of this Penny Jar situation:

2. How many pennies will be in the jar after 20 rounds?
   Show how you figured this out.

A Penny Jar Story (page 2 of 2)

3. Make a graph of the Penny Jar situation in Problem 2.

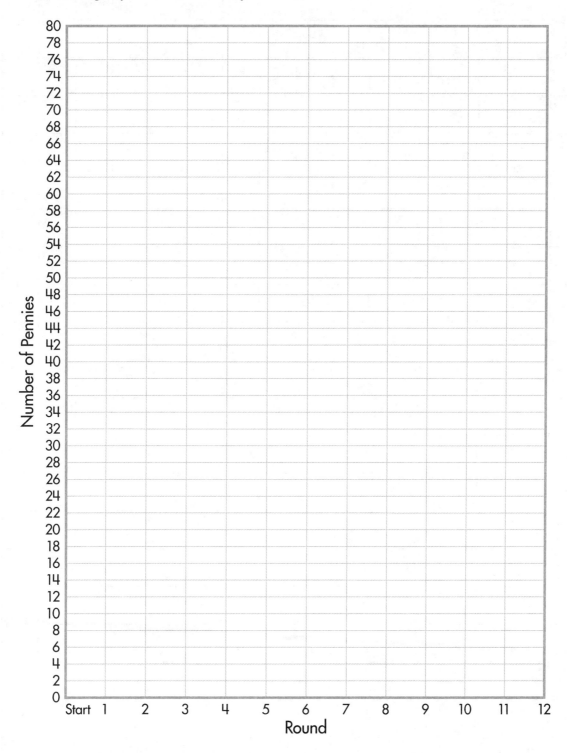

Removing Pennies
from a Penny Jar (page 1 of 2)

Here is a Penny Jar situation: Start with 95 pennies.
Remove 4 pennies each round.

1. Make a table to show what happens for 8 rounds.

Number of Rounds	Number of Pennies
Start with	
1	
2	
3	
4	
5	
6	
7	
8	

2. Make a graph of this Penny Jar situation on the next page.

3. When will there be 0 pennies in the jar?
Show how you figured this out.

Penny Jars and Plant Growth

Removing Pennies
from a Penny Jar (page 2 of 2)

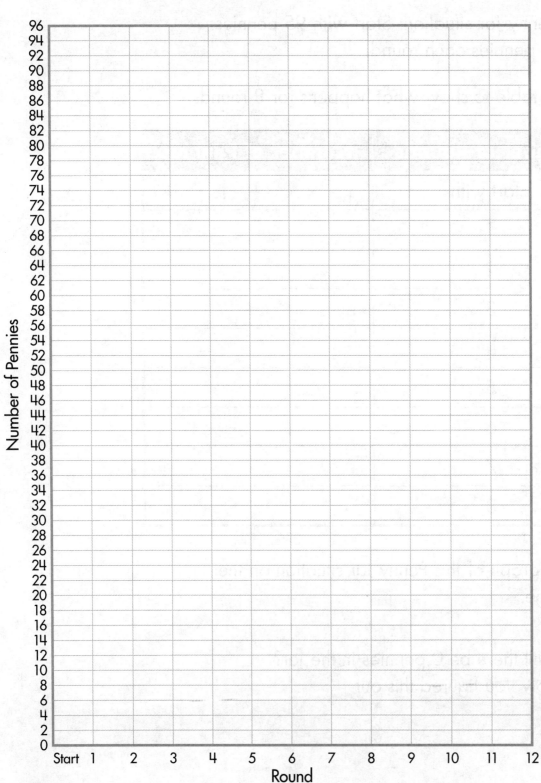

Number of Pennies

Round

Comparing Graphs

The pairs of graphs show plant growth.
Circle the answer to each question.

> **NOTE** Students interpret the shape of line graphs about plant growth.
>
> **SMH** 75–77

1. Which plant grew more quickly?

2. Which plant is taller?

3. Which plant had its top broken off?

4. Which plant stopped growing?

Ongoing Review

5. Which of the following is the most likely story of this graph?

   A. A Plant's Growth

   B. A Runner's Speed

   C. A Penny Jar Situation

   D. The Temperature on a Hot Day

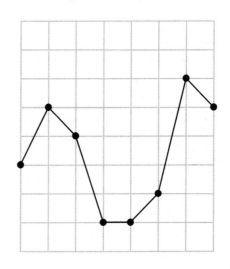

More Division Practice

Solve each division problem.
Then write the related multiplication
combination.

NOTE Students are reviewing division
problems that are related to the
multiplication combinations they know.

SMH 35

Division Problem	Multiplication Combination
1. 7)‾42‾	_____ × _____ = _____
2. 72 ÷ 6 = _____	_____ × _____ = _____
3. 8)‾48‾	_____ × _____ = _____
4. 108 ÷ 9 = _____	_____ × _____ = _____
5. 60 ÷ 12 = _____	_____ × _____ = _____
6. 36 ÷ 6 = _____	_____ × _____ = _____
7. 12)‾96‾	_____ × _____ = _____
8. 63 ÷ 7 = _____	_____ × _____ = _____
9. 72 ÷ 9 = _____	_____ × _____ = _____
10. 9)‾54‾	_____ × _____ = _____

Representing Constant Change

NOTE Students solve real-world problems involving the math content of this unit.

SMH 86

Steve earns $0.50 day for feeding his family's dog and making his bed. He wants to save $10.00 to buy some trading cards. He starts with $3.00.

Number of Days	Amount Saved
Start	$3.00
1	
2	
3	
4	
5	
10	
15	

How many days will it take him to earn enough money if he does his chores every day?

Write an arithmetic expression to show how much money he will have saved after 30 days.